The Other Woman at the Well

A Truthful Accounting of Addiction Overcome

By

Judith Ann Hillard

Foreword:

This is a book of rejoicing, yet in times of true rejoicing, it is first necessary that one experience nearly unspeakable sorrow. This I have dared to speak; the sorrow no one should see let alone survive. It is to and for the people who love me that I wrote this book, this tale, this tragedy, and this series of miracles. Read on, and you will know how undeserving I am of any form of grace. Long ago I threw myself away and decided that if He had any sense or good taste, God would do the same. Clearly, I am not qualified to comment on His taste or sense, but I can laugh uproariously at His sense of humor. And it is His humor which has brought healing back to my life, and I pray, to the lives of those who loved me through the unlovable, unspeakable times. Many of the names have been changed to protect the identities of those involved.

Humbly,

Judith Ann Hillard

Dedication:

This book is dedicated to Olivia Grace Hillard, without whom, after all, the miracles just wouldn't matter.

Reviews by others:

From a former student of mine, also a recovering addict and a teacher:

I wouldn't change a thing. It's about your experiences, your life. It is somewhat a sad, depressing depiction of what you have been through but at the same time, uplifting the way you have opened up in what you've written. You truly are an amazing writer. You look great, by the way, and I am happy to scc how hcalthy you have become. I was afraid for you the last time that we saw each other. You were so ill, so fragile. You, again, look like the Judith I know and remember. I hope and pray that you will remain on this path, clean and healthy.

From the husband of my first friend in years:

Judith,

Thank you for allowing me to read this. It is a miracle you have survived at all. Your writing is excellent. You are truly a gifted writer, as I am sure you are aware. I find your story fascinating. I have never been exposed to anything like this, the book writing process or the soul-baring story you are sharing with Jennifer that I have hijacked.

Again, thank you.

Troy

From my friends Mark and Mischelle, who have also lived the miracles:

Paraphrased: Mark and I read your work together. It is very powerful, Judith. Mark said your description of 8 seconds of happiness each 24 hours is exactly right. Keep writing Judith. You have been anointed with words. Use them and keep healing.

From my friend Jennifer, yet another miracle:

"You don't have to dedicate the book to me, Judith, but you do have to keep reading it to me. Write on, every day."

From Olivia's teacher:

"Judith, I love the title. Your book is well-written, witty, funny, and horrible all in one!

Audra White

From my Father:

Jude,

More to your story than I ever knew ... that is just as well. But, now that this old life of yours is PAST YOU and you and Olivia are finding the "true high" (LIFE) ... just keep writing and writing. The editing will come with the volume of past and ugly memories on paper. These words will most likely save scores of others from the "edge" where you have been, and don't want others to approach. In fact, I am visualizing the "sequel" ... the LIFE of Mama and O --- the wonderful life the two of you enjoy every day in your NEW LIFE without drugs!

You are loved. Your story is needed.

Love,
Dad/Opa

Table of Contents:

Chapter One: Life 101

"If you can't be a good example, then you'll just have to serve
as a horrible warning." (Catherine Aird)

"And He had to pass through Samaria. So He came to a city of Samaria, called Sychar, near the parcel of ground that Jacob gave to his son Joseph; and Jacob's well was there. Jesus therefore, being wearied from His journey, was sitting thus by the well. It was about the sixth hour. There came a woman of Samaria to draw water. Jesus said to her, 'Give me a drink...' The Samaritan woman therefore said to Him, 'How is it that You, being a Jew, ask me for a drink?...' Jesus answered and said to her, 'If you knew the gift of God, and who it is who says to you, "Give Me a drink," you would have asked Him, and He would have given you living water.' And she said to Him, 'Sir, you have nothing to draw with and the well is deep; where then do You get that living water?...' And Jesus answered and said to her, 'Everyone who drinks of this water will thirst again; but whoever drinks of the water that I shall give him shall never thirst; but the water that I give him shall become in him a well of water springing up to eternal life.' The woman said to Him, 'Sir, give me this water, so I will not be thirsty, nor come all the way here to draw.' (John 4:4-15)

Years ago I had a flip-page calendar aptly entitled "Sniglets." These were made-up words that appropriately described everyday things in our lives for which we had no name or description. For example, "Discombeebopulate: to turn down the music while driving, searching for a specific address;" or "Furnadent: the little indentations in the carpet that show you where to place the furniture after vacuuming;" or "Carperpetuation: when you vacuum fruitlessly over a piece of fuzz several times and then pick it up in your fingers and toss it down again to give the vacuum one more chance." I can even remember these: "Accordionated: the ability to fold a roadmap while driving," and "Musquirt: that yellow watery stuff that shoots out of the mustard jug ahead of the mustard." But my favorite "Sniglet" of all time was simply this: "Re: the middle stuff in an OREO cookie." I kept it thumb-tacked to the bulletin board in my classroom for years. It was only recently, however, that I found myself relating to it.

I am Re. I am sandwiched between a ten-year-old daughter, Olivia Grace (whom we often just call "O") and a mid-60s-year-old mother, Virginia Ann and father, Dale. It's funny that they were Mom and Dad for 35 years, and then the moment Olivia was born, they became Opa and Grandy even to me. So you see, I am truly a Re, sandwiched between two O's. The generations on either side of me seem to mirror one another in their fastidiousness about their hair and clothing, their beautiful friends and people they just seem to collect at church and in girl scouts and civic groups, like charms on mom's old bracelet, or gems on her new one. Me, well, I have certainly collected my share and then some of friends and beloveds, but have dutifully lost them one by one as I would have lost the charms and gems, if I'd had any to lose. I am not a collector, as is my mother, of the perfect table placements for each major and even some minor holidays, and the exact matching shade of shoe for each handbag and suit. I am not a packrat, as is my daughter, of every painting her hands have ever blended and every doll she has ever left naked beneath her bed. I am very neat, though. If I made only $200 per month I would gladly spend $100 of it on a house cleaner.

I was popular in school, with my peers, my teachers, the administrators, and my friends' parents. I earned good grades. I earned leadership scholarships all through college and graduate schools. I was even the homecoming queen at Arizona State University my senior year, much to the pride of my sorority sisters and my father. I was the third Delta Gamma in as many years to achieve that honor, (though I think there was a Kappa in the middle as well) and the second generation of women in my family to carry home that crown. Anyway, my life was easy, though I never realized it until it wasn't easy any longer.

Today I don't think of myself as the near-PhD that I am, or the Master of Counseling or Education or English that technically, I still am. I don't even carry the MS (short for multiple sclerosis) that forever changed my outlook and life about seven years ago and used to tag alongside my identity like another set of credentials. I don't define myself as the teacher or professor I was for over 16 years. Today I think not so much of my vocation, but of my avocation of the past 25 years or so and see myself for what I really am: a drug addict. Today I don't have to swallow or snort or smoke or shoot-up a drug to know who I am. Regarding today, I am grateful and I am clean. I intend to be so tomorrow as well. Hey, my best group meets on Friday nights and tomorrow is Friday. Besides, if I slip up, the O's on both sides of me will call each other and begin living together again and I will be left once more, all alone in my misery and emptiness and pain. I will NOT choose to allow anyone in, including the house cleaner, so my surroundings will not fit neatly into my motif. Blood will be splattered on my clothing and sheets, carpet and tile, and in a few weeks mysteriously show up in spots on the ceiling, the light switches, the mirrors, and the doorknobs INSIDE. I won't notice it for days, maybe even weeks.

The only staples in my refrigerator will be orange soda and pomegranate juice, which I will beg my sister or a neighbor to buy for me next time she goes to the market and then just set by my door (where I'll have taped a terribly hand-written check reimbursing and compensating said person). Today, that is not a place I choose to live. Today, that is not a place I choose to die.

I no longer have to step into that swamp to know that the alligators are still there, hungry, hidden beneath the otherwise unbroken surface, their teeth are razor sharp and they feed on the arms and legs of the sad, broken people who continue to reach into those waters, skimming for comfort or peace or at least an end to their pain. This I know as well as my name; I carry the scars. I have survived more alligator bites than I can describe. I AM the Velveteen Rabbit; my skin has all been worn (not loved) off. I doubt I will ever wear short sleeves again, and I live in Phoenix where 123 degrees is normal in summer and summer seems to last four or five months of the year.

It is almost impossible to know where to begin to tell my story. I could start, I suppose, with the separate yet related births of two babies, thirty-four and a half years apart. We were both big, robust baby girls who looked at birth, I am told, very much alike. I guess the biggest difference between my daughter and myself is that I began life with a mother almost as young and innocent as I was myself, at the time. Olivia began her life with me, a mother who has been, at times, too well loved, too well educated, too well accepted, and most certainly, too badly addicted to elicit simple description.

I remember having an insatiable curiosity about life all through my childhood, even reaching into my college years. If you were my teacher or the parent of one of my friends, I felt truly blessed to know you and have moments of your time and attention. It has sometimes surprised my parents that I have remembered things one or the other of them said or sang over forty-five years ago, but I can still hear their voices in my head as clearly as I did then, whether they meant each little word they uttered or not. I was a good student, and that fact made me a careful one. Probably because it carved out a definition of myself that made sense to me at the time and I did not want to alter it by failing to pay attention one afternoon or simply not caring so much the next morning. So each spelling bee counted with me, each touch of the volleyball, each column of figures.

T.S. Eliot once wrote of his character J. Alfred Prufrock that he had, "measured out his life with coffee spoons." That was me, to the grain, and I suppose such a structure, like a house of cards, is bound some day to collapse. At any rate, I did. And this is my story, though my living to tell it is, I believe you will agree, quite remarkable.

Chapter 2: Background

"Some mistakes are too much fun to only make once." (Miles Davis)

"The thief (Satan) comes only to steal, and kill, and destroy; I (Jesus) came that they might have life, and might have it abundantly." (John10:10)

In August of 1991 I stood in a semi-crowded reception room at an old Ivy League school, waiting to be introduced along with my classmates, as a new Ph.D. candidate. I had moved from Arizona, where I had spent most of my growing up years, to be there. I heard the professor begin what amounted to a very impressive introduction of a class of 12 doctoral and 26 masters students, considering that he had met each of us only once or twice and was using no note cards. I was directly across the room from the learned professor, and was therefore introduced about midway through his ad-libbed performance. "In the brown and white polka dot sundress," he motioned to me, "we are pleased to welcome from the sunny state of Arizona, Ms. Judith Ann Hillard. Ms. Hillard comes to us bearing the proud title of Homecoming Queen from Arizona State University, a campus of some 50,000 students. But lest you think her a bubble-head, let me also underscore that Ms. Hillard had the only perfect 800 analytical score on a GRE exam I have ever had the pleasure of assessing."

At that moment, I felt the weight of expectation crush against my spine. I had left my teaching job of several years and achieved what I considered the distinction of earning a place of study at an old and ivy-covered institution. But in that moment, I felt the eyes of all the other entering and continuing students in the room land squarely on my once tiared and probably pointed head. "Great," I thought. "Now all of the women in the room will hate me and all of the unattached men will make their way over here with proffered glasses of chardonnay and not-quite benign offers of showing me around the city."

If I had a dollar for every person, nurse, doctor, therapist who has said to me over the years, "How could this happen to you? You come from a good home. Your parents are still married to each other. You are smart. You are lovely. You are successful. How could you let this happen to you?" I would today be a very wealthy addict, but an addict just the same. "This" can happen to any of us on the planet. It is not reserved for poor black men under the age of 25 living in the inner city. It is not reserved for tired housewives over the age of 50 living in the suburbs. It does not live on skid row alone. I shall do my best to explain, indeed, how this happened to me and how I lived to survive it which is far more miraculous after all than the fact that I allowed it happen to me.

I was a preacher's kid, the president of both the National Honor Society and the Student Body of my high school. My classmates voted me "most likely to succeed." I doubt any of them dreamed that less than a year after I started snorting cocaine (which helped my life initially as I began writing my dissertation since I didn't need sleep, food, liquids, or even people), I had blown out my sinuses so badly that if I slept, I awoke the next morning feeling that my face was on fire. Often I awoke to the sound of myself sobbing in agony. I cannot describe the pain I endured and found, of course, the only numbing agent that worked was yet more cocaine. It reminds me now of that old Sambo story of the tiger running so fast around a tree, chasing his own tail, that he turned to butter.

In a way, I guess my classmates were correct. I learned very quickly to be a "successful" drug addict; once I was fired from my dream teaching job, I was able to use cocaine much more frequently. My life began to deteriorate rapidly when my nose bled often and the pain never stopped. My dealer knew I was in trouble and threatening to stop paying for his deliveries, so he offered to take me to Patrick, another of his "clients."

Let me insert a word here about drug dealers. In my opinion there are two types of drug dealer: the ones who use and will cheat you by adding baby powder, or Drano, or baking soda to the cocaine so that they can use more, and the ones who do NOT use and will cheat you in much the same way, or will just short you by giving you say $600 worth of coke when you have handed them ten one hundred dollar bills. In summary, do not trust drug dealers. The former look and smell terrible, but can somehow still weigh and count and calculate. The latter look and smell fabulous, usually with dark, slicked back hair, maybe pulled into a modest, short ponytail. They are both slimy, but in completely different ways.

Anyway, I love my father today all the more because he is not perfect, and because it took us both many, many years to accept this truth. We both expected perfection from him, would scoff at the absurdity of anything less. And I imagined myself to be just like him. I yearned to be perfect for him and because of him. And because I saw early that he was not perfect, I tried unreasonably to be so myself. If I got all A's, I would bemoan that there were not more A+'s, and expect him to do the same. In fact, I brought the A's to him, paying homage to our family ideal, underscoring our slightly skewed image of our perfect selves. Because perfection is not attainable by we mere mortals, I grew angry with my father. And because my father worked for God, at least on Sundays, I grew angry with God too. I had it all backwards; I thought they were both angry with me for letting them down.

I did not know at the time that the gift of grace was already at work in my life. I found out when it showered like a summer storm in Maine all around me, some months later.

Chapter Three: My First Encounter with Grace

"You may be only one person in the world, but you may also
* be the world to one person." (Unknown)*

"For if by the transgression of the one(Adam), death reigned through the one, much more those who receive the abundance of *grace* and of the gift of righteousness will reign in life through the One, Jesus Christ." (Romans 5:17)

One night when I was in my third or fourth treatment center in maybe 15 years, I got down on my knees beside the warped, curling, black and mostly white striped mattress of my assigned room and said this prayer, pretty much word for word:

"God, if you can still hear me, just give me a reason to live. I don't
     even care what it is."

I was 33-years-old at the time, a few months shy of 34. I had been fired the Christmas before that (for the first time in my LIFE, I'd been fired) from a fabulous prep school back east – from the dream job of any English teacher, having about a dozen students per class, and only four classes a day. My sophomore class was purely a poetry class. That's it: just poetry. Can you imagine a more idyllic job?

I knew not only my students' names and the names of their parents, but also their lineage (even teaching a young relative of Andy Warhol) and the names of their siblings. I watched them play lacrosse and field hockey on warm fall afternoons. I taught one of them to actually speak aloud without his classmates answering for him, and did so slowly, meticulously, by questioning him about what he'd had for dinner the night before (making sure ahead of time that no one in the class had been a guest at his table, and repeatedly making them all sit on their hands). Day by painful day that 15-year-old boy, Kevin, began to find his voice and use it; and his mystified classmates began to hear him for the first time in 10 or 11 years. Most of them had been students of the institution since pre-school (and had apparently been answering for Kevin the entire time). It was known in the yearbook as the $140,000 club, as tuition hovered around $12 - 14k per year.

The day they fired me I was only two hours late for the meeting with the headmaster and my department chair. One of them said, "What we're about to do is always so difficult."

I remember saying off-handedly, trying to bring a lighter tone to the gathering, "Meeting? What's so tough about that?" When neither of them answered, but instead attempted to pull their eyes away from one another and focus into mine, I remember asking "What is it, exactly, that we're about to do?"

I was missing only two or three days a week at that point in my otherwise truly unimpeachable career, but providing lesson plans for the substitutes (whether or not they were legible plans is probably at least another chapter's worth of explanation). When I was there, if I could not hit a vein in the women's restroom, I'd open a vitamin capsule and pour the powder into both sides of it, squeezing them together and using it as a suppository. You can believe me totally when I tell you that I never passed gas in the teacher's lounge!

One horrifying day one of my seniors pointed to my crisply starched yellow Polo oxford and said, "Ms. Hillard, you're bleeding!" I looked down at my left arm and watched the red circle grow from about a quarter to far more than a silver dollar. I had to go to the nurse for a band-aid, pressing the antecube area of my arm tightly, and then had to insist that she not clean nor see the wound as I had to get back to class. Imagine? I was appalled that they were firing ME, a gifted and award-winning teacher.

One day after lunch I stepped into a more public ladies room than the private one I frequented. There was probably about

½ inch of clearance between the door and the stall frame. I was busily injecting a syringe into my horrible looking, necrotic (dead) left arm when I heard the tap tapping of heels entering the room. I believe it was the headmaster's secretary who rather innocently looked through that crack and uttered a guttural gasp that chills me (and probably her) to this day. It was only two days later that I was called in for the "so difficult" after school meeting. I was angry with her for a long time for telling my secret to the boss. She may instead have been one of those earthly angels who conspired to save my life.

I wrote to Kevin that next year, though it took me nearly the full year to do so, and my deadline was his graduation from high school. Most of that letter has disappeared from my files and journals, but here is what I have left of it. It was an answer to a letter he wrote, thanking me.

30 May 1995

Dear Kevin:

As I begin, I must tell you that along with this letter comes an assignment, custom-designed for you. I guess I am, hopelessly and forever, a teacher. This task may challenge you, but should not be as difficult now as it would have been the fall we met, when it might have been unthinkable. If you learned anything in my class worthy enough to carry with you throughout life, I hope it was confidence. Perhaps I helped you find and believe in your own voice, both in your writing and speaking. But it is your voice, one you have possessed yet withheld most of your life. Kevin, you have much to say. You write thoughtful, meaningful, appropriately humorous poetry. You are bright and insightful, if somewhat reluctant to let others know all this about you. And the letter you wrote me articulates a sensitivity and kindness most men, most women, and most children (especially adolescent males), never know. You pay attention to life, as do all good writers. Don't waste any more time, Kevin. Use your voice. Speak it always.

Shout your words from the mountaintop, "Oh Captain, My Captain." Make your life extraordinary. I know you can.

Humbly yours,

Judith Ann Hillard

Chapter Four: Patrick

"Experience is a wonderful thing. It enables you to recognize a mistake
*   when you make it again." (Unknown)*

"What then shall we say to these things? If God is for us, who is against us?" (Romans 8:31)

Patrick, it turned out, was not only a cocaine addict, and as I was about to learn, heroin addict as well, he was also a physician at Penn (where I, too, was a grad student). He led me to a bathroom up the stairs in his far-more upscale row home than mine. He brought out his black satchel, instructed me to take off all my clothes (which I refused outright for a sinus exam) and shined a flashlight up my nostrils. His diagnosis was simple, "You can't snort this stuff anymore. You have nearly deviated your septum."

"Yeah, right!" I exclaimed. "I need this stuff. I have a dissertation to write," as if no one had ever done so without the aid of illicit substances. Patrick seemed to understand this flawed logic and calmly explained to me that I didn't have to stop USING cocaine, I just had to change my method of delivery. I honestly couldn't imagine what he meant. He explained that cocaine was most effectively delivered to the body in the same way his hero, Sigmund Freud had used it, by injection. "I don't think so," I protested, backing away from him, his bathroom, and the syringe he pulled from his bag. "I'm a preacher's kid from the Midwest; I am not a junkie."

"What could happen?" he asked me.

"Well, for starters, I could die," I said, as if he were a rather simple pre-schooler not understanding the most basic concept of color.

But his answer is etched forever in my memory. "I'm a doctor. I could bring you back."

"Hhhhm," some sad, sick part of me contemplated. "I guess I could give it a try then, but I don't know how to do it."

"Not a problem," he smiled. "Remember, I'm a doctor."

This was a Sunday night, September the 8th I think. I was to begin a new teaching job the next morning, but it was early evening, so I wasn't concerned about tomorrow yet. Well, Patrick had to be the clumsiest doctor I've ever met. He was like Gerald Ford, tripping down the stairs of Air Force One. But somehow he managed to concoct a brew in a spoon, light a fire beneath it, twist off a wad of cotton from the end of a Q-tip, and suck the brownish yellow liquid into his syringe through that cotton ball. I made sure it was a new needle, not wanting to get sick or anything. (How crazy a thought is that at such a moment in one's life?) As I allowed this stranger to push the drug into my vein, I felt my neck go tingly numb, and then my ears began to ring, and I felt a euphoria envelop every cell of my skin, brain, and heart. I can only describe the trip as pure perfection, as if I'd flown into the night sky and taken a bite of the moon itself.

The next conscious thought I had was this: "Wow! What time is it?" It was my favorite time on a digital clock beside a bed I don't remember lying upon. It was 11:11. Very neat and orderly, like thin soldiers lined up in a regimen. The problem was, I didn't know if it was morning or night, Sunday or Monday. I panicked at the thought that I was already over three hours late for my first day of teaching at the academy. I awakened a nearly comatose Patrick who was lying on the floor not far from me and we quickly turned on the television to discover the eleven-o'clock Sunday news was on.

"Yippee," I thought. "I can do this again." And we did, over and over again throughout the night. I was late for school the next day anyway as I had Patrick drive me home so I could shower and change, and then drive me to school. We went to the wrong campus, it turned out (there were two) and I slinked in to the correct one carrying a huge travel mug of coffee and an L.L. Bean backpack. It was chapel and the sanctuary was full and formal, to put it mildly. The only open seat I could find was in the very first row. I had missed the breakfast and socializing hour and perhaps 20 minutes of the opening worship service and felt terribly conspicuous as I smiled my way into a room of curious observers.

Patrick was supposed to collect me at 3:30 from the original campus that first afternoon. He did not answer either his phone or pager and I waited on the front steps for nearly two hours until he finally arrived. Drug addicts are not the most punctual nor reliable folks on the planet. About this, they do not care.

It was days later that I learned Patrick had added heroin to the mix, which lengthens the high of the cocaine and slows the heart so one doesn't accidentally die (at least not usually). It's called a Speedball, and though I weighed only about a hundred pounds at the time and had never used heroin in my life, I did not die. But John Belushi, probably 2 ½ times my size, did. So it is not a foolproof method, even if there is a doctor in the house.

I wonder now how Patrick intended to save me after he'd given himself a shot a few moments after mine and promptly passed out? The question bothered me many times, but I did nothing about it. For the next two months I lived in a chaotic, desperate place; I tried to teach and sleep and sometimes hydrate myself with a popsicle or a bite of tuna when I was feeding some to my cat. Usually I found a lukewarm purple puddle saturating the paper of the popsicle. Then I would just slurp it up and toss out the stick and paper. Very rarely did I need to use the bathroom, but by the time I realized I needed to empty my bladder, it had already started to do so without my consent. Often the only time I changed my clothes was after I'd wet my pants.

Patrick had what seemed like an endless supply of pills for pain, nervousness, sleep, or any controlled substance you could think of. It turns out he had once interned in an AIDS clinic and knew they stocked these medications, along with AZT and other scheduled drugs. So, he simply contacted a pharmaceutical supplier and set himself up as a clinic, at his own address. I found this rather stupid, and told him so in the same lecture I gave him about missing two consecutive weeks of work (I know, am I the pot or the kettle?). I feared he would not just lose his license to practice medicine, but would face criminal charges if the legal drug supplier realized he was a person, not a clinic. Still, I helped myself to his mountains of pills. They did help you "come down" after spending several days "up" on cocaine.

I learned quickly how to inject myself, always careful to use clean needles (even if I just licked them off, they were mine alone). One night I had prepared a 4 mg shot in one of the fat syringes Patrick had delivered. I set it alongside the bathtub and took a nice hot shower, hoping a vein would appear. One did, in my thin leg, which I noticed while drying myself. I reached for the syringe and actually hit the fat vein I miraculously found in my left calf. The needle had clotted while I showered, but the vein was too good to give up on. So, I just pushed the clot through and all 4 mgs of cocaine and heroin (at least four shots worth for me at the time) immediately raced into my bloodstream. I tried to step out of the tub, but fell flat on my face, cutting my forehead and chin on the cabinet, unable to use my hands to break the fall. I literally crawled like a baby on my knees into the bedroom and tried several times to lift myself up to the phone on a bookshelf.

I was not trying to overdose but I had. I lost the involuntary ability to breathe and somehow called Patrick and begged him to come over and help me. I was terrified; I could barely speak and my heart was hammering even in my eyeballs. My cats were going crazy walking on me, standing on my chest, "screaming" into my mouth and nose.

I was supposed to drive over to Patrick's house that evening for a party. When I told him what happened and begged him to come over he said, "It wouldn't be worth the trip. You'd be dead by the time I could get there." I was horrified. To his credit, he did explain that I was going to have to remain conscious and make myself breathe; he would help me through the phone. I have no idea how much time passed, but I remember his voice screaming my name a few times to wake me. And I remember him counting to three or six and then demanding that I breathe. I did as he said.

Some hours later, I dressed myself and decided it was probably best not to drive, so I called a cab to take me to the party. I licked a red popsicle as we drove, not noticing that it dribbled down my face and hands and into my clothing. I think the driver noticed, however, as he kept staring at me through his rearview mirror. I would smile at him, attempting a normal tilt to my head and an easy-going nature. I must have asked him thirty times if we were almost there yet. I was four and two hundred and four all at the same time. Patrick and his friend and sometimes housekeeper Charmaine (though what she "kept" other than her extensive drug habit is still a mystery to me), had started the party without me.

At one of their parties, the first time I met her in fact, Charmaine would not leave the upstairs bathroom. She thought there were bugs crawling just beneath the surface of her skin and would not stop digging at them with her filthy fingers or stabbing at them with her equally filthy needles. Patrick assured her numerous times, as did I, there simply were no bugs. There may well have been hallucinations crawling throughout her body and mind, but they were not insects. Patrick gave her some kind of special shampoo and instructed her to use only one capful. It may have been lice shampoo or something like that. I had essentially tuned her out by then, as she could be quite annoying. Anyway, I was talking to her about my cats when she fell quite suddenly and loudly to the floor. This woman perhaps tipped the scales at 90 pounds, and was remarkable in appearance only in that she was covered with tattoos all over her body that resembled railroad tracks, criss-crossing all across the nation of Charmaine. I later learned these junctures were places she had once unearthed viable veins. Her train tracks had been well traveled.

Charmaine used to borrow Patrick's car to go collect the heroin. One night she was gone for way too many hours. He had grown furious. When she finally called, it was to tell him that she'd gone outside the drug house to find his car had been stolen. He was never quite sure if that was the truth, or if she had simply sold it for more drugs. He sent a cab for her and was more annoyed by the delay than he was by the "theft."

Anyway, one evening she crumbled to the floor and began seizing. Even I, the non-doctor, could see what was happening. Not one part of me, however, wanted to touch her nor hold down her tongue. I was paralyzed with fear that she would die. Patrick stood there like a rubber-necker at a train wreck. I had to yell at him that he needed to help her. "What do I do?" he screamed.

"You're the doctor! You said you could bring us back. Get to it. She's dying." Charmaine had already wet her pants and her body was bouncing up and down on the dirty floor as her tongue, swollen, was lolling around her lips and her too-well shampooed head was banging against the tile floor. Yet, Patrick remained frozen.

I told him I was going to call 9-1-1. Well, that catapulted him into action.

"NO!" he screamed at me. "Get me my black bag."

I did, and then feeling as if I would vomit, I left him to her. I went to his computer and tried to look up seizures and heroin overdoses and the weather in Shri Lanka. Anything but listen to him begging her to breathe, breathing for her, crying, weeping, wailing. Patrick was very worried about how he would either explain to the police how his cleaning woman had mysteriously died in his home, or find a way to dispose of her body. No matter how beautiful the weather along the coast in Shri Lanka, I could not help but hear his ramblings and confusion. I prayed for sanity to return to his house as fervently as I prayed for Charmaine to return there as well.

It seemed like a very long time, though it was probably just minutes, when I heard Charmaine's voice come around. She remembered nothing about what had happened and thought Patrick was trying to kiss her. Hey, he may have been in his clumsy, bumbling way. Yet, he had saved her. It was more the fear of police and firemen that motivated him, I must say, than it was the fear of her death. He sickened me. They both did. I couldn't wait to get out of there.

I discarded Patrick on November first that year. He was really weird and always thought I should have sex with him in exchange for his generosity with drugs and sodium chloride bottles and clean syringes. Of course, he was far more an addict than he was a lover. He never even climbed stairs after he started using and I knew that, so diverting his flimsy seduction attempts was pretty simple. Still, I was tired of the bartering. I told him to never call me nor come by again. He didn't, though sadly, I had not heard the last of Patrick Ford, nor of Charmaine.

I used IV cocaine by itself and by myself then, as I had no other heroin connections and was terrified of the neighborhoods Patrick found that sold the little blue heroin bags with clever sayings stamped in red ink upon them (names like "Stay Up Late," or "For a Great Time" or even, outrageously in Philadelphia "Brotherly Love"). I came to think of them as the fortune cookies of the drug world. Who cares about the cookie anyway? It's what's inside that matters. Dime bags, they were called, though they certainly cost far more than their name indicates.

I used IV drugs for exactly six months. It took only four for my arms to swell into footballs and then my skin to fall out in black clumps the size of a various citrus fruits. If I really concentrated, I could see some of the bones in my arms. It was much harder to find a vein.

Chapter Five: Traveling home

"Don't cry because it's over: Smile because it happened." (L. James Harvey)

"Abide in Me, and I in you….If you abide in Me, and My words abide in you, ask whatever you wish, and it shall be done for you….Just as the Father has loved Me, I have also loved you; abide in My love." (John 15: 4, 7, 9)

I flew home to Phoenix for both Thanksgiving and Christmas that year, 1994. I kept a four-day-stash of cocaine in the toe of my cowboy boot and carried pre-loaded syringes in my backpack. I remember "occupying" the bathroom in first class (though I was flying coach) for about 2000 miles, shooting up through turbulence, seatbelt sign warnings, and the incessant knocking of fellow passengers and flight attendants. Why I was not arrested for transporting over a pound and a half of cocaine across state lines, I'll never know. And what judge on earth would have believed me when I explained that I was NOT trying to distribute illegal substances? I only brought enough for my own private consumption over the holiday weekend. I had well over a thousand dollar a week habit in only a few months as a junkie. I was still employed at that time. It got worse.

I had not slept in at least ten days by the time I got home, and I stayed up all night Thanksgiving Eve doing drugs in my parent's guest quarters. I managed to stop and shower and stick up my hair with mousse before the meal. My father prayed and I joined the long table of my parents, two of my siblings (the youngest had just graduated from high school a few months prior and our brother had just begun taking classes at a local community college where I later taught public speaking and business communications for a number of years), and my maternal grandparents. I ate small helpings and then went immediately to bed for my Thanksgiving nap. I awoke sometime Saturday morning only to find my parents talking to their physician friend, Marlin. They had gone through my things as I was unconscious in the room before them. They found my drugs and my frightening supply of bloody needles and syringes and little glass bottles of sterile water. I sat on the couch, feeling defensive, but unsure why. Marlin kneeled before me and quietly asked me to roll up my sleeves. At first I refused, looking at both of my pale and frightened parents standing behind him, craning their necks to see how bad I really looked. I've already mentioned that my skin had turned black and had begun to fall out in clumps, maybe like a leper in Calcutta. Finally I did as he asked and rolled up the sleeve of my "good" arm. Marlin hung his head and big tears fell down his face. He made no attempt to wipe them off, but continued to cradle my arm in both of his hands. He asked quietly if he could take me to the hospital right then, but I refused. He explained that the infection in my skin was called cellulitis and was probably already in my bloodstream and maybe even my heart. If I did not go with him right then, I would certainly die. There are two facts here that I must explain. One, I was not finished with cocaine at that point and two, I did not care what happened to my body. I had already thrown myself away. I explained that I had a plane to catch the next day and classes to teach the day after that. I could not possibly check into a hospital 2500 miles away from a job I'd just gotten a few months before. It was, after all, a great job.

The other thing I remember about that day is my mother's reaction. My father sat very still in his leather recliner. I don't know if he wept or not. My mother turned instantly on her heel and marched quickly into the laundry room off of their huge country kitchen. I heard the most horrible wailing sound I have ever heard coming from her direction. It was as if she were infected and dying. I asked my father what she was doing and he explained, "Your mother is grieving the loss of your skin. You do this to yourself, you do it to her." As a daughter, I thought they were all being rather melodramatic. Looking back upon it now, as a mother, I cannot imagine the agony my parents felt when I rolled up my sleeve and they saw death zigzagging its way down the arms and legs of their first child; their superstar; their straight-A, homecoming queen, most-likely-to-become-the-first-woman-President daughter.

I caught an earlier flight the next day. I returned to Philly and my job. I was fired less than two weeks later, on December the 12th. I was generously given a three-month severance package and allowed to keep my health insurance. The headmaster urged me to go home to Phoenix and let my family help me with whatever it was that was wrong. I drove back to Grey's Ferry intending to pack up and move home. Instead, I sat and bled on my sofa full-time. I don't remember much about the Christmas break; only that once again I refused to go to the hospital, and I insisted I had to return to my row house and finish packing. I caught a much earlier flight that time.

Chapter Six: The Angels

*"We could learn a lot from crayons: some are
sharp, some are pretty,
 some are dull, some have weird names, and all are
different colors...
 but they all have to learn to live in the same box."*
(Unknown)

"Do not fear, for I am with you; do not anxiously
look about you, for I am your God. I will
strengthen you, surely I will help you; Surely I will
uphold you with My righteous right hand." (Isaiah
41:10)

The ensuing months in Philadelphia were unremarkably the same. My insanity grew as did my daily use of IV cocaine. The morning passed without my permission as two of my friends carried out their responsibilities in order to deliver what was left of me to my parents 2500 miles away. My flight was scheduled to leave Philadelphia at 8:30 a.m. that February the 7th, 1995 and arrive in Phoenix roughly five hours later. I had missed a flight three days before, and one the week before that.

I could not be trusted to get myself packed, or transported to the airport, or even out of the bathroom where I had resided for several months. Neither could Chase, who wanted me better, but also wanted to be the one and only who got me there. His efforts were earnest, yet futile. My occupation in those months was IV cocaine addict.

Prior to that I had been a teacher, a daughter, a friend, a sister, a Ph.D. student, a human being. Once again, I did not wish to be on the airplane. I did not want to leave my bathroom. I had long since forgotten who I was supposed to be in the world or who

I used to be. I lived only for the next shot, the next high, the next lift-off to what I experienced as a trip to the moon.

Stepping out of my shower that bleak, cold February morning, I weighed 84 pounds. I was 33-years-old. I had to bandage my arms and my legs so the necrotic (dead) tissue, blood, and pus would not seep through my clothing. I carried 12 loaded syringes in my luggage, though I had used most of them and the loaded parts that remained carried mostly my darkened blood, in hopes that I had sucked back enough of the cocaine coursing through my bloodstream that I could try again later, once the plane landed in Phoenix, and hopefully find more success in getting that ecstatic rush at home than I had in Philadelphia.

I traveled that morning with one small pet, Louisa May Allcat, who had become my lifeline. I had rescued her several months before from the alley behind a row house I rented in the ghetto of Philadelphia. I was in such bad shape that my friends walked me all the way onto the airplane, helping me strap the seatbelt around me and setting Louisa's small cage directly beside me. I saw one of my friends talking to a flight attendant and gesturing toward me and though I don't know what was said, I know the employees of that airline looked worried and rather gray whenever they approached me throughout that flight. They were probably afraid I would collapse before the plane landed. Maybe they were afraid to take their eyes off of me. I know that when I took the heavily sedated Louisa from her cage and held her on my lap, no one scolded me.

When I awakened later, Louisa was back inside her cage and the very large, black businessman seated in my row was petting her head. Louisa was never stowed away beneath the seat. Maybe it was obvious that I needed to feel her fur and hear her purring so that I could keep breathing. Maybe I was finally willing to stop fighting everyone and everything.

Two months earlier, when I had flown home for both Thanksgiving and again for Christmas vacation, I had spent the majority of those flights in the airplane bathroom shooting up drugs. That February morning, however, I never left my seat and am not sure I could have walked if I had. I was very weak and had not eaten in at least a week. I had not slept in five days and the last liquid I'd had was the puddle that remained of a grape popsicle that had melted on the bathroom countertop the night before.

My parents met the plane and took me immediately to Good Samaritan Hospital where we were met by a team of specialists awaiting us in the emergency room. An infectious disease specialist, a cardiologist, a heart surgeon, a general surgeon, a plastic surgeon, an internist, a kidney specialist, and several others examined me. They worked as a triage unit to prioritize which parts of me to restore in which order.

First it was determined that they had to keep me alive in order to begin to repair the damage six months of IV cocaine usage had exacted on my body. The first surgery occurred the next morning wherein they placed a Groshong catheter in my heart in order to deliver IV antibiotics into my bloodstream for the next six to seven weeks. This was to be just the first step, however. I remained in their care for the next seven weeks, surviving several surgeries and four weeks on the burn/trauma unit as they debrided my wounds and soaked me twice daily in huge water tanks to keep the infection from destroying what was left of my limbs altogether.

The skin grafts were harvested from almost all of my left buttocks, which hurt far more than my battered arms. For some reason that made a great deal of sense at the time, I refused to allow the surgeons to remove any skin from my right buttocks. I wanted some part of me left unchanged/untouched. As if on a beach it would matter how my right cheek looked in a French bikini. The level of pain changed when I was transferred to the burn unit where they dry-packed what was left of my arms and legs and then ripped that packing off twice a day. Huge amounts of morphine, Demerol, and Dilaudid were pumped into my white line (and huge amounts of blood were drained from my red line as they tracked my various infections and blood counts), but nothing eased the torturous pain. The nurses then applied a cream called Silvadene that actually completes the kill of dead tissue, and sent me off far too often to physical therapy where they floated me in what looked like huge stainless steel horse troughs, all 84 pounds of me hovering precariously like my hospital gown upon the surface of that water and then ripped the packing off again.

Medical personnel were endlessly stepping into my hospital room and asking me if I could sit up and take a deep breath. I recall that I could not. My hemoglobin count had fallen, overnight, to two. Most AIDS patients die if theirs dips to four.

We didn't need to hire Monk to discover what had happened, though I'm quite sure the physicians never knew what happened that afternoon in the PT lab. My skinny body, like the thin hospital gown billowing around me, bobbed on the surface of the water of my physical therapy tank as my youngest sister Jaime and my friend Sally stood beside me, overlooking the procedure. The surgeon had instructed the physical therapist, Karen, not to use any tweezers, scalpels, or instruments whatsoever as she cleaned my wounds twice daily after the whirlpool soaks. He told her that they had debrided right up against the main artery in my left arm, and that the slightest nick could pierce that thin vessel and cause me to bleed out.

Karen, a bit of a cowgirl and know-it-all, to put it gently, had not listened to him. Each hour in her chamber was punctuated by excruciating pain. One day I even passed out cold from the pain and that was after she has sent for my nurse to bring me yet another 150 mgs of Demerol so Karen could keep playing "doctor" but not in any fun or nostalgic way that I could recall. There may have been enough narcotic in that hospital to kill me, but there was not enough housed there to kill my pain.

That particular afternoon, my third or fourth back in Arizona, as she hooked me into the harness, lowered me into the bubbling water, and returned to her desk filled with paperwork, my 18-year-old sister and dear friend screamed her name, "KAREN! Get over here. The tank is filling with blood!"

With each beat of my heart, pint after pint of blood was draining from my frail body, filling the tub. The last thing I remember is hanging there in the harness, suspended inside bright red water, losing more and more of my consciousness with each beat of my poor, exhausted heart. Karen hopped into the tank beside me, drenching her uniform and pressing my artery closed with all of her considerable strength. She yelled to my sister to grab a towel and carefully climb into the tank. She instructed my baby sister on how to tie a tourniquet onto my upper arm, but I could still feel the painful pressure of her hands around my fresh surgical wounds and see her uniform turning red just before I passed out.

While "playing doctor" she had inadvertently sliced open that weakened artery. Mysteriously, it was never charted. No one knew why or when I had lost so much blood. I awoke sometime later in my hospital bed with a vague recollection of Jaime crying and telling me good-bye. I don't think my sister ever thought she would see me alive again. If sitting up to breathe had been difficult the first week of my confinement, it became impossible after the blood-filled horse trough.

One less-than-friendly nurse, hanging one of my packed blood transfusions, answered my inquiry of "what's wrong with everybody today?" by explaining simply, "You're dead honey. You just don't know it yet." I told her I'd be damned if I'd give her the satisfaction of dying on her shift (hey, she was really slow with the pain shots anyway, so risking offending her was not really problematic in my mind). I honestly believe that glimmer of determination kept me breathing until the shift change the next morning.

One of the many miracles that saved me was the fact that a cocaine addict had personally impacted the lives of each of my three main nurses. The mean one had recently thrown her son from their home after he had stolen money, small appliances, and then beat up his father. My day nurse had buried her identical twin in the year prior to my arrival. Her sister died of endocarditis due to IV cocaine use. Kelly, that nurse, told me I looked like her sister, only sicker, at the time of her death. She begged me to live, explaining that she just could not go through it all again. The night nurse had lost a child to addiction. She held onto me as if she couldn't bear to lose another.

After that, I can't tell you why I lived. I had not yet uttered that 11th hour prayer to God. I did not yet care whether or not I lived nor died. To complete the story, I must return to the academy, when I stopped by the next day (after they "let me go") to gather my things and say good-bye to my students. It was second hour, poetry class (my favorite) and it was that small boy Kevin who silently stood and carefully held onto his rep-striped tie as he climbed onto his seat and then the attached desk and saluted me, "Oh Captain, my Captain." I still tear up as I see his thin face, his determination, his strength of character and know that he went on later to become the editor of both the school newspaper and the yearbook. Kevin found his voice, wrote spectacular poetry, and celebrated his gift for words right out loud. It is, however, a good thing I did not remain there as his captain for my ship was already sinking and as the mean nurse pointed out, I just didn't know it.

I think I accomplished only two good things that year. The first was helping Kevin to find and use his voice. The second was this little cat, barely four pounds after I'd been feeding and coaxing and cooing to her for four months in the alley behind the ghetto where I lived at that point. It really was the ghetto. My teacher and grad school friends were afraid to drive in broad daylight to my house.

A friend of a friend had purchased the 200-year-old row house, right across the street from Tiny's Tavern and a couple of boarded-up, tagged by gang symbols indecipherable to perhaps anyone but the gang members themselves, crack houses, because it was affordable (like $60,000, I think) on her social worker salary and then found herself too afraid to live there. I had been paying over $1200 a month for a one-bedroom apartment in the suburbs when my friend offered me her friend's house for only $300 per month.

I had moved in the same week they offered it to me, honestly afraid of nothing by then. I figured I was scarier than anyone who might have the nerve to bust into my house. All I'd have to do was roll up my sleeves and show them the blackened wounds and exposed bone that I could see in a few places. My arms had long-since stopped feeling pain. But even I could see that they looked excruciating, like I'd suffered full-thickness burns and had not yet had the good sense to have them treated.

When I walked past my telephone I could hear my mother and youngest sister talking to each other, in Phoenix, about me. I didn't even have to pick up the receiver. I could hear them. When my friend Chase (the drama teacher who saw me at the faculty picnic that first day and decided I was destined to become his) would come by to cook and try to feed me, both he and I would hear each other's voices in that rickety old house. He would trudge up the stairs and beat on the bathroom door (I spent hours in the tub searching for a vein, which made clean-up afterward quite a bit easier) and ask me what I needed. The thing is, I hadn't called him but he had heard my voice beseeching him to come upstairs for a minute. The same would happen in reverse as he called me to the laundry room in the basement, or the kitchen on the first floor.

Annoyed beyond belief, I would wrap what was left of my body in a big terrycloth robe and march down to him, "WHAT? Why did you call me?" He would look at me with this blank expression and explain that he had NOT called me. He had been humming some show tune and never broken stride as he marinated the salmon or shish-kabobbed the filet.

We started calling them the "ghosts," those voices we heard frequently in my house. I could see the heads of my cats following their discernible, creaky footsteps on my old, cracked, wooden stairs as they climbed up or down. I never saw them, but I frequently heard the distinct voices of two women (one a bit older, one young, perhaps still in her late teens or early 20s) and an older, wise man in those months.

One day in the tub I heard them communing outside the door. The young woman said to the wise older man and woman, "She's calling us the ghosts." The man explained with a touch of laughter, "Well, at least we know she can hear us." From that moment on they became to me (and to Chase), the "angels." Months later I told my sister Jan about the angels that lived with me on Grey's Ferry Road in Philadelphia, PA. She said quite matter-of-factly, "I know. Billy and I prayed in each room and corner of your house the morning after you left to teach, asking for angels to watch over you in every room of your house. We were afraid you would die there."

Chapter Seven: Louisa May

"Life may not be the party we hoped for, but while we are here we might as well dance."   *(J. Williams)*

"Yet those who wait for the Lord will gain new strength; They will mount up with wings like eagles; They will run and not get tired; They will walk and not become weary." (Isaiah 40:31)

Anyway, about the cat. One condition of my affordable rent (leaving far more of my budget available to purchase cocaine) was that I would feed and help rescue the many strays that lived in the alley behind my thin house. All but one of them were tomcats. One huge yellow Tom had weathered a terrible brawl, leaving him with a scar that circled his entire head, making the fur on top look like a cheap wig. I named him Toupee. My friend ended up adopting him, as ugly as both he and his voice were, as she knew no one else ever would. There was one tiny little calico girl whom I later named Louisa May. The second good thing I did that year was sit patiently in my postage stamp backyard at a rickety picnic table some generation ago had abandoned there and wait for the boys to finish snarfing their food, as Louisa did the same. I bought a cat dancer, which she badly wanted to play with until she would realize that my hand was on the other end of it. Gradually, painfully, day-by-day she would come a little closer.

Side note: my brother was sent to visit me there in the ghetto. One night as my next-door neighbors shot at each other during one of their daily brawls, he hit the floor so fast I nearly wet my pants laughing. He wanted me to turn off all the lights in case they were shooting at us. Anyway, he caught sight of Louisa sprinting away from him and from then on always said she "took off like a shot." I guess he knew of what he spoke after spending a few days across the street from Tiny's Tavern. By the way, she was perfectly named, as she was about as big as Louisa May. I could differentiate between them, however, as Tiny always had a half-burnt down cigarette with about 3 inches of ash dangling precariously from her pinched and wrinkled lips. Louisa did not smoke.

The first time I ever touched her she was perched atop my cinderblock fence, eating without fear and I ran my hands lightly down each side of her thin frame. At first she jumped back in terror, and then she wiggled down and purred, almost like saying, "What? How dare you touch me?" and then "Ooooh, that feels really nice." I promised her then and there that the next day I would pet her again and pick her up. I would carry her inside and take care of her for the rest of her life (or mine, whichever ended first). It was a God thing that I rescued Louisa May "Allcat" from that group of raping monsters. You see, to fatten her up, I fed her tuna from a can. I always remembered to feed her as well as my other cats (and sometimes in so doing remembered to feed myself, if only a bite or two of the tuna). I had at the time three other cats: T.S. Eliot, Nikki Giovanni (who was black, as were all of my neighbors – I was known simply as "that white girl"), and Henry David Thoreau who had settled into my fireplace when my crazy animal rescuer friend Carmen found him as a kitten and brought him over, months before addiction ruled my life. "Look," I had said, "he's returning to the woods for reason and strength."

"You're keeping him," she smiled knowingly. Name them and they're yours was Carmen's philosophy though I steadfastly refused to keep Toupee. He was even uglier than me, and nearly as tall when he stood on his hind legs and attempted to open my back screen door, bellowing for dinner the second I got home. It was a happy day when Carmen carted all 30-some pounds of Toupee away. It was a blessed day when I carried tiny Louisa May Allcat inside my house. She hid for three weeks, though I knew from her empty plate that she was eating and using the litter box in the basement. I literally had to show her how to live inside a house, that it was okay to sit on the sofa with me. A week or two later as she tentatively climbed each step to the second floor, that it was fine to jump on my bed and sleep with me (by then I was only sleeping about 3 days every two weeks, and so soundly then that I did so all at once and could not be awakened). I had driven her to the vet to be fixed and get all her shots, but was too comatose to pick her up. She came home in the backseat of a Checker cab. It cost me as much to transport her as it did to pay the vet.

My ghetto neighbors were the best I've ever known. Hortense, who probably kept binoculars at both her front and back windows (none of us had side windows, as the row houses were all attached to each other), kept vigilant watch over the neighborhood AND the neighbors. She knew intuitively that the third year resident whom I thought of as my friend for a few months, and who would steal clean syringes and saline for us when he worked hospital shifts, but was too paranoid to drive and so took cabs to my house and squinted in all directions as if the DEA itself were on his tail, was bringing me drugs. She watched the cats disappearing from the alley, which was a good thing in her mind. She also watched me disappearing right before her eyes and actually called my friend Carmen to tell on me. Carmen then called my parents.

Chapter Eight - My Return Home:

"A truly happy person is one who can enjoy the scenery on a detour." *(Anonymous)*

"By this, love is perfected with us, that we may have confidence in the day of judgment; because as He is, so also are we in this world." (I John 4:17)

My father enlisted Carmen's help and Chase's to get me onto that plane February the 7th, 1995. Without Carmen's strength and determination to keep me alive, Chase could not carry out the task himself. When I would accidentally overdose, Chase would invariably be asleep and miss it entirely. I don't know if it was the work of the angels, lending me his involuntary urge to breathe, or if I simply wore the man out with my escapades and his attempts to keep me alive. Carmen thought Chase a nuisance, at best, and totally inept at getting me packed and loaded onto an airplane. If we'd been in the Wild West (and in a strange way, we were), she was a marshal who came to town with pistols blazing, armed for combat. I was boarding that coach, no matter who tried to stop her. Anyway, on the designated morning, they arrived about 5:00, maybe four hours before we had to leave for the airport to make sure I was packed, my drugs were not, and my animals were all crated for the trip. I carried Louisa May aboard, as a carry-on. I was so ill that the airline allowed my friends to walk me onto the plane and I saw Carmen whispering instructions to the flight attendants and pointing to me. I don't know what she said to them and I guess it really doesn't matter. I think they just breathed a sigh of relief that I slept the whole time and did not die in flight. They didn't even stop me from taking Louisa (doped on one of my valiums for the flight) out of her tiny cage and cradling her in my arms. We both slept soundly all the way across the country.

My enormously relieved parents met me at the door of the plane and we went straight to the hospital. My dear friend Sally kept my cats all of the next many months, until I had an apartment in the Phoenix area and she gave back three of them. Nikki had become Sally's during my convalescence. Louisa never liked any human except for me, and was smuggled up to my hospital room by both Sally and my Episcopal priest friend, Phoebe, months later, when she had come for a visit and I was back in the hospital another time. It worked out, though, as Phoebe had never been to Arizona and she commandeered my old Saab and my apartment and got to see the state "with the huge sky" as she wanted.

Chapter Nine - Jody (the Phoenix dealer):

"If not for STRESS, I'd have no energy at all."
(Unknown)

"…for God *sees* not as man sees, for man looks at the *outward* appearance; but the Lord looks at the heart." (I Samuel 16:7)

As soon as I was well enough to walk, about five weeks into my hospital stay, I went to the ATM at the hospital and withdrew $400. From a pay phone in the lobby I called Jody and begged her to take a cab to my hospital room and bring me $300 worth of good cocaine. The extra hundred was for her. That did it. It was a long day as I waited for Jody to arrive. I had been saving syringes in a pillowcase I kept inside the air conditioning vent in my bathroom. My IV line was a needle-less system, and over the weeks the nurses had not been careful to put every syringe and saline bottle into the locked red box on my hospital room wall. Often they tossed them into my bedside trash, or just left them on the nightstand. I continued to collect them, eager to use in the Groshong. I wouldn't even have to find a vein.

When she finally arrived, I had Jody shut the door and promise me that no matter what happened, she would stay with me and count and NOT let the nurses in. She was true to her word, but it had been several weeks since I had used and never had my heart received such a powerful jolt since the drug had to travel only about two inches. I was catapulted backward into what may well have been a seizure. I could no longer hear my heart beat, though I could hear the alarm on the monitor attached to my body going crazy. Jody looked horrified and I could barely hold up my fingers in a gesture to remind her to count out loud. One finger. Two fingers. Three. Finally she complied and with all the strength I had, I made myself take in and then release air. A couple of nurses came flying in the room, demanding of Jody, "What happened? She was fine and now her blood pressure is 210 over 170." I don't remember what happened after that. Jody left, begging me to be careful. The nurses never asked me what I'd done. I learned to follow Jody's advice and be more careful. I shot drugs into the very lines the medical personnel were using to save my life. I was resigned to it, but not happy that the residents had to remove the central line the day they released me. I knew it would even more difficult to find a vein since I was now covered with bottom skin all down four limbs. I was alive, but I wasn't finished yet.

I asked Sally to bring Louisa May for a visit. One day, she finally smuggled her in. I held her for hours and stroked her fur. She purred and seemed relieved to find me again. Together we napped. Some time later a nurse pitched a fit after finding an animal in my room. She scolded Sally, but only after I'd been visited by a stand-in plastic surgeon who announced himself as "Doctor FawnsWorth." We have laughed over the soap opera entry of that man many times. Later she took Louisa home with her and left me a two-pound box of my favorite candy in the world, Mary See's nuts and chews. The nurses had eaten most of my first box when I was in surgeries and treatments. This one I horded and only rarely shared, and then never with nurses.

One of Louisa's hairs somehow got inside my IV line and settled up against my heart, causing me a fever of nearly 106 degrees. After that the nurses put the kibosh on any feline visitors. Somehow, the cat hair passed (as do most hairballs) without causing me a heart attack or another systemic infection. I suppose God just wasn't finished with me yet. He was awaiting that prayer and his miraculous answer to it.

Chapter Ten - A Letter of Hope from my Father:

"Wisdom enables one to be thrifty without being stingy and generous without being wasteful."
(unknown)

"This is the day which the Lord has made; Let us rejoice and be glad in it." (Psalms 118:24)

February 23, 1995:

Dear Judi,

It is now 4:39 AM and I am again awake and decided to write you another letter (I have no idea where to find his earlier ones). This seems to be the time when I do that best. The Pennsylvania letter was written at about the same time. I admit this Arizona letter makes me feel a lot better knowing that you are here and in the hospital getting better each day.

The key, my dear, is you. You are more and more appearing the Judi we all remember. It is good having you back – by that I mean "having you back." You went away from us for a while, and away from yourself. I truly believe you are day-by-day getting back to all of us.

The surgeries, the skin grafts, the healing process has begun. This phase cannot be easy for you. I see you moving steadily forward and am most Thankful for this process. I am pained to see you hurting; it is painful to see, but I know it is part of the healing process. I am watching you progress; see you become more interested in life on a daily basis. You are buying laptop computers, ready to communicate with your fingers, even with pressure garments on both of your arms! You have much to say. You are eager to say it. It is clear you cannot write it longhand. I can attest to that! Judi, I am so happy to see what you have to write now.

Mom was describing to me the movement in your left arm. It seems to me the key for you will now be physical therapy (remember, I nearly lost the artery and therefore, the arm – Venus de Milo, I feared, was one of my soul sisters). Let me urge you to take full advantage of your hospital benefits and work that opportunity to the fullest extent at this time. Don't try and rush the process. Take time to heal. Remember, it took quite some time to get you here, to this place. It will undoubtedly take at least as much to get you out of this place. Face the physical therapy and stretching of your arm in the hospital or treatment center where you can gain the additional 30 or more days for both separation from the opportunity to further abuse cocaine and the chance to obtain full use of all four of your limbs. While pursuing these matters, you will be able to write and try out the capabilities of this newly acquired computer. (It was a charge nurse in Chandler who, ignoring the dresser shoved against the door with that old portable Apple upon it, who sent it crashing to the floor one afternoon when a "friend" brought me a supply from Jody. I threatened to Sue them. They never replaced my computer and my words typed into it went into the same garbage heap where it landed.)

Focus on your healing first; establish the goals we have mentioned, but have not written yet; then align them to your priorities – one of the things you do so well and now that you are coming back will get once more into proper perspective (see what I mean about his insatiable optimism?). Don't try to take on more than you should in this return to normalcy. It was through our first encounter with you and AA that we learned to take things "one day at a time." You must do so now. Sally will welcome you into her home, but I think 30 days in therapy will be vital to your physical and addictive healing.

I like talking to you and seeing the progress. You will carry scars as clear reminders of where you have been. I believe you will not wish to return to this place again. I fear that you will be given opportunity to return again. Are you aware how close you were to the edge this time? One cannot continue to live on the edge. No one is that sure-footed, and the danger is certainly not worth the risk. The need is not in playing at the edge. The need is to stay near the center. The family and the friends and God are in the center of your life – stay near them (us) for we are your strength and in reality, you are a part of our strength. Trust in the bond that exists for us all within the center, near one another. Come back from the edge, my dear one. It scares us all too much for words to think of losing you.

Judi, welcome home. Judi, welcome back. I love you.

Affectionately,

Dad

Chapter Eleven - My Parents Say Good-bye to Me:

"Only those who will risk going too far can possibly find out how far one can go." (T.S. Eliot)

"And let us not lose heart in doing good, for in due time we shall reap if we do not grow weary. So then, while we have opportunity, let us do good to all..." (Galatians 6:9-10)

I had been out of the hospital several weeks before I began using again. I was in no program. I was attending no meetings. Of course I used again. Sally threw me out of her house the first time I didn't call or come home one night. Jaime and her friend drove to Sally's to retrieve my things. Sally was true to her word. I had a home there as long as I stayed clean. I lived with her almost a month.

I didn't really have a place to live after that, at least for a few weeks. I stayed sometimes with my parents, other times with my local dealer, Jody, in her hovel of a one-room apartment, or in a hotel. It was one of Jody's regular customers who called my family and told them where to find me. They alerted the management to my condition and after I'd been inside the room three or four days, the evening manager knocked once and unlocked my door. My mom, dad, and little brother stormed inside. Mom checked to see if I was okay. I was, ironically, as I had slept for much of the four days. My dad began packing my things. My brother nearly broke my arm as he twisted it behind my back asking where I'd hidden the drugs. I did not answer him so he began tearing the room apart in search of them. Clever as I was, he found the 28 ounce bag the addict had told them I had (please don't mistake his call as kindness or concern for me. I'm very sure they had run out of money and cocaine at Jody's and decided it would be brilliant to bust me to my family and then come and get my drugs). I took the drugs with me.

We went to the ER at St. Luke's Hospital where I had 11 years before that successfully completed treatment. I let the ER check me out and mom tossed the still-heavy baggie into the trash outside the door. I refused, however, to let them admit me and explained to my family that it didn't count if THEY threw away my drugs. I would just get more. They knew this was true. I found the bag in the trash and pocketed it. My bag was already packed and instead of going inside their lovely home, I kept asking them to drop me back in south Phoenix.

Finally, my dad turned the car around and drove me as close as I would let him to Jody's neighborhood. I could not run the risk of letting them know where she lived. As he pulled my rolling suitcase from his SUV, my father reached for me and held me tight. He said good-bye to me that night, certain they would never again see me alive. He told me it had been a great honor being my father and he loved me. I watched until his taillights disappeared and then dragged my suitcase to Jody's.

Chapter Twelve - The Prodigal Daughter:

"A breath of kindness is more moving than a gale of flattery." (unknown)

"I can do all things through Him who strengthens me." (Philippians 4:13)

One afternoon, after a hefty overdose, I called my father from the Emergency Room and asked if he would come and sit with me. He did. I remember him holding my hand as they pumped oxygen into my lungs and monitored my heart. "Dad?" I asked him, when I could talk, "Was the Prodigal Son's dad mad at him when he came home?"

His eyes crinkled as he answered. I think he was smiling and crying at the same time. "Oh yeah, he was furious. But he was more happy and joyful that his son had come home than he was mad that his son ever left." Of course, we were talking in code about us, not about a parable. I knew the face of God and his limitless grace in that moment, in the face and words of my father. He had called every friend of mine he could think of, begging them to come see me in the hospital and help him make me choose to live. He was terrified that I would die. For him, I wanted to live. Once more, I just didn't remember how.

I don't know if they admitted me then or not. I know I had over 30 operations over the next decade, beginning with the debreding and subsequent skin grafts, and then the insertion of implants exactly like those used for breast cancer patients who've had mastectomies. Every week the summer of 1996 the plastic surgeon would add more and more saline into my eight implants, therein stretching the skin in all directions, hoping he could stretch enough to remove the grafts and leave me with four to six thin scars. This worked on my legs. My arms, however, turned out to be keloid. I healed fast and scarred worse, like those kids whose vaccinations in the sixth grade grew into golf balls and stayed huge. No matter what I did, or what pain I endured, I remained a marked woman. I remained scarred by cocaine. I couldn't figure out why God would save my life only to let my body stay ruined. I prayed many times for Him to remove my scars. If He answered, the answer was unequivocally "No!"

I moved into a two-bedroom apartment in Chandler, about eight miles from my parents. My friend Chase packed all of my things and rented a U-Haul to drive them out to Phoenix. Dutifully, he helped me unload and move into my apartment. Finally I had the freedom to use in private once again. I was all set up (yeah, for failure).

Chapter Thirteen -What I know of Insanity:

"Vision is not enough, it must be combined with ventured. It is not enough to stare up the steps, we must step up the stairs." (Vaclav Havel)

"The one who guards his mouth preserves his life..." (Proverbs 13:3)

"Hello, Your Hair is on Fire!"

Here is a letter I wrote while using cocaine. There were moments of clarity and even brilliance while using the substance, just as Patrick had told me there would be. Unfortunately, they usually came and went so quickly that I couldn't quite remember them, or if I'd written them down, I couldn't read my own handwriting in order to recapture my brilliance. This time, I'd written at the computer, in the form of a letter to my friend in Pennsylvania.

Dear Carmen,

I just realized the bathroom was filling with smoke and a horrible smell because I had leaned over a candle to soak up some cocaine-juice that had spilled from my spoon, and my hair caught fire. The hideous, burning smell competing with my nostrils was my own scorched hair. It now looks sort of the opposite of a Mohawk. Before I had the presence of mind to stick my head in the tub, it had pretty much burned me down to 1/2 inch of peach fuzz, forehead to neck; a virtual runway down the center of my head. It took off most of the hair on my back and left a couple of charred places on my neck and shoulders.

Hello? Anybody in there? YOUR HAIR IS ON FIRE!!

I kept thinking it was one of the more realistic hallucinations I'd ever had. If so, it had touched upon all five senses. That's when I started to panic.

As I came in the den and sat at the computer to get this down, I was letting the bathtub fill with water to better soak my scorched head. I went to check on it just before high tide washed me away. A wall of water was pouring forth from the bathroom door, coming down the hall toward the den and this computer. I didn't think it had been running that long.

I haven't slept since Easter Sunday, the day I missed church, breakfast with my family, four phone calls, and dinner with that same family. I didn't hear a thing, and the telephone was right by the bed, next to my head. I've eaten only three or four popsicles in the past four days. I don't think I've left the bathroom in two. My hands look like puffy plastic doll hands. My hair is gone. I've ruined my arms and legs. I can't even lay out by the pool again. It is very difficult to believe that I'll ever have a life again. Baldness will certainly improve my appearance, don't you think?

This is not a hallucination. There are at least two inches of water on my bathroom floor. It is so high it has filled the bottom of the trashcan. At least I don't have to worry about cleaning blood off the floor any longer. Nor will I have to worry about blow-drying my hair in standing water. I have no hair. The damage is asymmetrical. The candle was on my left. So the left side of my head, by my ear, looks as if it is, well, "receding." Or it looks like I was on the Kansas side of Oklahoma yesterday morning. I was, I'll have you know, the only person in the western hemisphere who didn't know a thing about the bombing until late afternoon (on my Grandparent's television when I noticed an official-looking newscast in a non-news time. "What's going on in Oklahoma?" I asked.

"What? You don't know. I've been in surgery most of the day and I heard," remarked my grandmother. "There was a huge explosion this morning in a Federal Building in Oklahoma City."

I don't pay much attention to the media when I lapse into a common sense coma. Of course, why subscribe to secondary news sources when one can tap into a main artery?

I do so well for a week or two, and then, unexpectedly the thought, "Hey, I could call somebody and get some cocaine. Nobody will know" hits my sluggish brain and I essentially absent my soul for a day or two, until the coke runs out. If it hasn't been much fun (and this has not been, in case you were wondering), I get really depressed and disgusted with myself and see no way out. That's when I get more. You'd think it would be the other way around. Sometimes, it is.

I don't know who I am anymore. I don't look or act or sound like me. I honestly want to die, Carmen. If I don't, I guess I'll call Janis and see if she can start with my hair and then move on to fixing my head.

When I go into Automatic Addict, every ring of the phone is a threat. Every voice and sound I hear in my head (I'm not saying anyone else can hear them) is incentive to leave the bathroom and peek out the vertical blinds. It's always you or my parents that I fear finding out. If the doorbell actually rings, it can't be you of course, as you are in Philadelphia and I in Phoenix. Sometimes it is my worried and frantic mother, often with a foil-covered dish in her hands that I can see through the peephole. I never answer the door.

If any of you call, the game is up. You can hear cocaine in my voice. I can fool pretty much everyone else. Now how am I going to keep the charred remains of my hair a secret? Hmm? I called 9-1-1 and asked what one does when her hair is on fire. They replied, "Ma'am, are you okay? Do you need us to send a team out to you?"

"NO!" I cried. "I just need to know how to stop the burnt places in my hair from continuing to fall out."

The calm, probably confused emergency operator was the one who suggested I submerge my hair, but also explained that if it was truly burnt, only time would bring it back. Was I certain she couldn't send me some paramedics? I was certain. I put my Penn cap on my head where it remained until the next day. It was with great fear that I stood before the mirror and lifted up that navy cap. Imagine my surprise when I was not nearly as bald as my father. Of course, on a lighter note, he always says that grass does not grow on a busy street. To back up that argument, my street had certainly not been a traffic jam the night I burnt my hair.

Sometime later I wrote: Just wanted to get this little document out to you. Though much of the drama was hallucination, I did burn a few holes in my hair, and some places are now short and fuzzy where they should be long and chic. (Oh well.)

Much Love,

Judith Ann

I also found a copy of the letter I wrote to Phoebe, the dear friend I made through no particular talent on my part in my few months at the prep school. It is Phoebe who helped me that fall when I was mad at God and feeling so very alone. I asked her if she REALLY believed Jesus was dead for three days, or just in a very deep coma from which he later emerged, having been pulled off the cross? Did he REALY raise the dead, or just know some early form of CPR? I'll never forget her answer, which became a turning point for me. "Judith, if I'm going to stretch my very human mind to attempt a grasp at the mind and heart of God, if I'm going to believe in Him, then I choose to believe that he can do really cool things." That was it. No preaching. No deep theology. Just cool things.

"Why not?" I thought. I can believe in cool things. I started to that day, and little by little, month by month, that seed of faith grew and broke ground with me. Today it is a "tree, planted by the water." It shall NOT be moved.

12 April 1995

My Beloved Phoebe,

Where shall I begin to explain to you what I know of what went wrong, or crazy, in me? What words could I possibly find to express my gratitude for your cards, your wisdom, your kind, peace-filled words?

I have agonized over this, and this is my thinking to date:

The yearning for cocaine is greater than any need, any longing I have ever known for any one or thing with the sole exception of my yearning to find ecstasy in God. It is true, Phoebe. I cannot remember how I once felt connected to God, or to my own life. And I have been starving to recapture that lifeline. It is the same hunger, somehow. It is equivalent, but it is down here on earth, or perhaps even lower. It is tangible, obtainable (albeit expensive as hell, literally), but reachable. It is the yin-yang. The dark side of this craving exactly parallels the light. As far below the surface of life as I have traveled is how vast a height to which I aspire. These are two identical sisters within my soul who thirst for enlightenment. As much as I have needed cocaine, I have needed God more.

Ah, perpetually, I remain the woman at the well, seeking the wrong reserves of strength, of sustenance. But still seeking!

So many times I have reached out and hesitated just before I brushed your sleeve with the perilous secrets that have haunted my soul, torn apart my body, my mind, my bank account, my self-worth. In those moments, I gave into the fears that had become my constant companions and lost faith in my belief in your honor, your wisdom, your love and courage. I worried that this was just too much for even you. This nasty little grimy secret would exceed your limits of acceptability. It exceeded mine, and it was happening to me, or at least to the shell of the woman I once was (forgetting, in those moments, that you were a product of the 1960s and therefore more tolerant than I'll ever be). In those fears, I shrunk away, I am ashamed to say. Yet, even in the midst of this terrible, weighty conflict, I knew *you* were the water. I consciously knew if **ever** I was to partake in the peace you spoke of, I would have to cast off my pride, my ego, my certainty that I would lose everything (and that list included your friendship, my job, my fragile sense of security, the confident, assured self I *believed* I projected to the world) and bear my soul to you. I'd have to (pardon the Protestantism) immerse myself in the still waters I always saw so clearly in you. In spite of myself, and my subsequent reluctance to entrust you with this mountain of troubles, I lost (almost) everything anyway. That list reads as follows: my job, my health, my self-respect, and my stupid, phony "world-face." Yet, if I read your words and thoughts correctly, I did not lose you. Incredible. Oh yea, and I kept (thus far) both of my arms.

You are my hero, dear Phoebe. I hold you close in my heart (fractured though it still is) and look forward to the day when I can look into the depths of your eyes and meet them with MY eyes. Eyes that are clear and bright and focused, able to look within as doggedly as they see without.

Someday you must copy for me (if you kept it) the original woman at the well letter I wrote you last autumn. I wonder if I was able then to express the great famine for God that rumbled in my belly? Somehow I knew you could show me the way. They say the teacher will be provided when the student is ready. As clearly as if Mother God pointed a spotlight directly on your face (and your collar), I knew you were to be my teacher from the moment I first saw you sitting on that stage at the Devon campus, the first day of school. The student in me stood at attention. The child ran away and continued to suffer, alone.

I apologize, Phoebe, for not trusting you enough. For not trusting the God I so longed to know enough. I shall try never to repeat that same mistake. My soul cried out to yours in such anguish. Did you hear those cries? Did you know that in the weeks and months we shared, I was facing what I hope have been my darkest hours? Did you recognize that I clamored to the light I saw burning so clearly in you because I had no light of my own? You once said you thought I was arrogant. If only you'd seen that I was nothing but terrified. Every moment of every day and nearly every night, I lived with my own jagged and tortured soul.

Come to the desert and walk with me, Phoebe. Allow me to send you one of the two free tickets I earned by "frequently flying" back and forth across the country. Take a long weekend, or longer. Come when you finish the school year. I need your guidance. I need to pray with you and, this time, touch your sleeve. I am fighting something bigger than lupus, bigger than cocaine addiction. I am fighting the distortions in my mind that have controlled my life in the past year. I am facing my limitations, my anger and shame, the reality of what I inflicted upon myself. I am facing my massive fear of death, and realizing I have an even greater fear of LIFE. For one full year I stared death in the face nearly every day, refusing to speak to or be shaken by it. "I grow old, I grow old...." T.S. Eliot wrote. But I, I do not grow wise. I know wise people. I am shown the way to the teachers, but I do not show them that small but central part of me that fears she is unloved and unlovable if she is not perfect. I have spent my life constructing faces with which to capture and entertain the students, the relatives, the people in charge. I have become a master of disguises. And now I am stripped of these costumes. I am naked, unprotected, and afraid. I have become unrecognizable to myself. I don't know what to do next. I don't know who I am. Why must I hurt myself so badly in order to learn what others seem so effortlessly to accept? Why can I not give up the struggle?

I realize this probably doesn't sound like much of a vacation for you, but please consider flying to the southwest. Please help me learn to live again. Show me how. We'll drive my new (old) Saab to the canyon. We'll hike in the desert. We'll harmonize with the guitar. Maybe Louisa May will even present her face to you. Now THAT would be some kind of miracle.

When I see her little furry face and think of what I nearly succeeded in doing to myself, I am so ashamed. I would never have injected her small helpless tiny body with cocaine. Yet, I inflicted it on me -- the only human being she has ever trusted or allowed to touch her. (She is attempting to sit on my hand right now. I guess she is helping me to get this part right.) If I had died by my own hand, Louisa May (and Eliot, and Nikki, and Henry) would have had no home, no person to care for them. I realize this sounds melodramatic, but I have needed as much to get my stubborn attention. This small creature tugs so at my heart. She has touched a place as no one, except you, has done in all of these dark months. If, for no other reason, I must choose life so that I might sustain hers.

It is complicated by the fact that I have honestly forgotten how to just live. Maybe I never knew. No one ever taught me how to BE a grown-up. I must have been absent that day of parochial school. To be perfectly honest, it just isn't as much fun as I had hoped. When I knew this was all there was, I lost hope. And then I lost that connection to God, to myself, to life. I just floated, aimlessly trying to find meaning by obtaining a Ph.D. Ridiculous. I nearly earned it in time to have it carved into my epitaph. Anyway, there is MUCH I need to hear from, and secondarily, say to you. I would love to see you and hold your dear face in my hands. I hope you will fly to Arizona and join me on this journey, if only for a few days.

You won't recognize me. I have gained 29 pounds!! I have set up a new apartment, plugged in my computer, attempted to adjust to a body that carries four skin grafts (long sleeves, long pants, no direct sunlight -- not an easy assignment in the "Valley of the Sun"), tried to reconcile myself to a future in this body, in its damaged and marked condition. I try to appreciate, oh, little things like water and oxygen and gravity. Things I took for granted or did not allow myself to enjoy for far too long. But still my soul thirsts. Please come to the table, my friend. Together lets prepare the feast and enjoy it. Show me the way. I know you know it. Teach me to live without argument, to give of my true self without fear. Please help me, Phoebe. I need you, and I **know** this. I just don't know how to convey it to you. You are one of my miracles.

It is so BIG to think about, but I have been amazed and humbled by my intense and immediate affection for you -- and that is a poor word for it. Nothing and nobody inspired or moved me in all of 1994 except for cocaine, Phoebe Killhour, and little Louisa May. I needed you and she. I **had** to know you both. I **had** to gain Louisa's trust so I could save her so SHE COULD SAVE ME! Miraculous, you see. My own little Clarence the Angel who jumped from the bridge on which I was perched, truly believing everyone would be better off if I were dead, or had never been born.

[Sidebar]: The entire seven weeks I spent in the hospital, Louisa spent hiding beneath Sally's bed. (I brought her with me on the flight from hell I took on the 7th of February.) Almost every day we were apart, I longed for her. She thought I had abandoned her, and I guess I had. She grieved and she hid. But she is very forgiving. She loves me far more than I love myself or deserve to be loved. If I cannot sleep, she does not. She sits with me. She sits ON me. She purrs. She smiles (I swear this is the truth). She did these things throughout the dregs of my addiction. Somehow, her need for me refused to let me die. Yes, Louisa May "All-Cat" knows how to live. And I know for a fact that, even as a stray in an alley behind the ghetto, she was living better than I. At least her survival instinct was intact. Mine had disintegrated. She ate when she was hungry, even if she found it in someone's garbage. I could not even feel the bitter hungers that accosted me.

Anyway, I have been the undeserving recipient of so many miracles, Phoebe. You cannot believe, for instance, how many of my nurses in those seven weeks opened up (many for the first time ever) about the sons and partners and sisters and grandchildren they had lost to cocaine. They took me into their confidence and expressed their pain and anger and loss, and they did so at a time when I could do nothing but cry. I have made up for years of not weeping since February the 7th. Anyway, now I am beginning to be able to write and talk about it myself. Maybe that is the answer. Maybe my life was spared so that I could sort out and then tell this tragic, painful story. Maybe my experience and words (you know I have plenty of those) will help someone else and prevent even more loss of limb and life and spirit. I loved these strong women. And I had no choice but to let them take care of me. They were so pleased as my strength and coloring returned. I guess I was gray when they brought me, my parents I mean, from the airport to the emergency room. I understand that I lost two quarts of blood in the first operation, and that they held staff meetings to prepare my family for what they considered my certain death. I just did not compute that I was so ill. It's not that I thought I was doing great, or anything. I just did not see the damage and death in my own self.

This reminds me, thank you for giving blood for me. The transfusions of four other people's blood literally saved my life. I could actually feel LIFE entering my bloodstream. I sat up in bed a little higher. I took deeper breaths. I had no idea how physically depleted I was until they began to drip four healthy pints of blood into my veins. There have been no accidents here. Of this I am certain. It will make a believer of you. [That was a joke, my friend.]

I think it has all begun to make a believer of Chase, but that is a tale I am far too weary to tell. He probably saved my life this winter, after I lost my job and began to work on my addiction full-time. He also nearly cost me my life by holding me hostage in my own illness (and his consuming neediness) in January. I am beginning to learn of the many big liberties he took when I was unable to recognize or prevent his "ministrations." I am angry with him. I am annoyed with his "phone-voice" and pandering to my parents and siblings and friends. It is like he has taken on this mission to manipulate all of my relatives into falling in love with him because he knows I am not and never will be. I am grateful for his kindness. I have grown tired of his childish obsession with me.

He read my journals and letters and secrets as he packed up my life in Pennsylvania. He returned phone calls that came for me. He appointed himself as my spokesman. Although I tell myself he is harmless and merely pesky, I have begun to feel victimized by a part of him I have only seen glimpses of. He will do such things as call the Arizona Department of Education and inquire about certification here, as if I have granted him permission to move to what has been my life-line, when I have pointedly told him that he will never share my bed nor my life. It is like this blind motivation that compels him to win a non-existent "Miss Congeniality" contest. As if suddenly I will acquiesce and anoint him Mr. Judith Ann Hillard. To be perfectly honest, he frightens me, Phoebe. No one falls in love so quickly. No one finds the madness and bloody carcass of a drug addict so attractive. It is not love. It is pathological, I fear, but it is not love. It's like his addiction to me mirrored my addiction to cocaine. I wish him no ill will. I think he needs some serious help, and I <u>know</u> I do. I didn't want to get into this; not in a letter. But I would welcome your counsel on the matter. See? There is so much I need to discuss with you.

Well, I am once again falling captive to my fears. I am afraid you will not believe me; afraid you will not wish to visit me nor Arizona. I even hesitate to ask this of you. I feel very undeserving of your time and trouble. (That fearful part is, I guess, the part that allowed Chase, the needy boy, to take over control of my life. I thought it was all the love I would ever have, even though he, alone, has called it love.) But, in spite of my fears, I am compelled to ask you anyway: Will you come to Arizona? Will you let me send you a ticket? (This will not be a financially expensive trip at all. Spiritually, however, it carries a hefty price tag. Although, I already have the gift of your blood. What more can you lose?)

I miss you, Phoebe. I miss the friendship we might have shared if I had been healthy and present last fall. I have grieved the loss of my students in a profound way. I have grieved the chance I lost to work with and know you.

I am tired. I shall try to phone you soon so that we can talk. It is my hope that this letter (sorry it is such a back-breaker) finds you healthy and happy in your new Monday through Friday home.

Much, much love to you, my friend,

Judith Ann

PS. I am enclosing my first feeble attempt to explain how it feels to be so addicted when you want so to be free. Note: it is rough, and not quite IT. But it is a start. Bye for now.

Chapter Fourteen - An Attempt to Explain the Madness of Cocaine Addiction:

> *"If all our misfortunes were laid in one common heap whence everyone must take an equal portion, most people would be content to take their own and depart." (Socrates)*

> "Be anxious for nothing, but in everything by prayer and supplication with thanksgiving let your requests be made known to God." (Philippians 4:6)

Never have I needed or desired a person or a thing with such desperation as I have cocaine. It is a thirst known only in part to those who wander unprepared and unprotected in the desert. It may begin as a walk of curiosity, in the relative comfort of the early morning. By noon, if one has walked far enough, and there is no water, the throat tightens, the breath quickens, the nostrils bleed, the mind dulls. By mid-afternoon, one collapses to her knees, crying out for mercy, pulling weeds from the earth to suck the gritty roots. By evening, when the heat has somehow amplified rather than diminished, and the crawling and the crying are no longer possible, one lies, face down, on the parched earth. The fear once felt about slithering, poisonous creatures has evolved into a kind of twisted acceptance. To this one, alone, whose skin blisters beneath the punishing desert skies, the thought of venom coursing through her veins brings with it the exotic hope of hydration, and the thought becomes logical. A thirst this great, for which one would gladly trade a limb or any earthly possession, is a drop of cherry Kool-Aid in comparison to the rancid sea of need one embraces after she walks into the vast and wicked wasteland of cocaine.

In fact, even knowing the Kool-Aid is laced with cyanide, the thirsting addict will lovingly, with trembling hands, press the red liquid to her own lips. She will partake of the poison cup. She will die if she must if only she can quench the bitter thirst.

Only one who has pulled his leg from the steel jaws of a shark can imagine the hunger for cocaine. Even the fragments of skin and bone and flesh that remain, proving the insatiability of the beast and man's unequal struggle in the watery home of his predator, are still not enough to keep the cocaine addict away from the shadowy depths. He believes it is he who feeds on the shark, though he loses more of himself with each encounter.

If you fear the darkness, you learn to carry a lantern. If you have lost the ability to distinguish between night and day, the lantern illuminates nothing.

If it is fire you fear, you learn to protect your home and alarm the children entrusted to your care. You form an escape route, post it, run practice drills, and pray you never need them. If you then pour gasoline around the perimeter of your home and still defy
the very fire you most fear, you have begun to glimpse the insanity of the great combustible, cocaine.

It is a madness unknown to those who have never listened to voices echoing in the empty corridors; the voices that grow more familiar, more believable, than the voices one has heard throughout a lifetime. If you cannot hear or have not spoken with voices whose forms you have not seen, if you have not traded the friends you once had for the unseen demons with whom you commune, your mind cannot accept the catechism of cocaine.

The only psychosis that parallels these is, I think, the belief that the fingers of cocaine cannot twist themselves into your own hair. To think it cannot touch you or someone you love is perhaps the greater insanity. Yes, your hair, too, could catch fire. And you may have struck and tossed the match.

Written 13 April 1995

Chapter Fifteen - A Cry in the Dark:

"It is when we forget ourselves that we do things that are most likely to be remembered." (unknown)

"Trust in the Lord with all your heart, and do not lean on your own understanding. In all your ways, acknowledge Him, and He will make your paths straight." (Proverbs 3:5-6)

I wrote a lot, looking back, in those months I was trying to heal myself. I went occasionally to 12-step meetings and did my best to tell the truth. I had not, however, surrendered my will and my life to a power greater than myself or greater than cocaine. At the time, I wasn't sure such a power existed (greater than cocaine). I knew everything to be greater than me at that point. I had practically given up. Yet I wrote the following letter to a dear friend of my father's, in response to a few letters he had written me, knowing the anguish my father was feeling. They had known one another since college, since before I was born (though just barely) and my father must have shared with his lifetime friend his fear of losing his eldest daughter.

12 April 1995

Dear David:

As I have begun this letter at least a dozen times, I have variously taken you into my confidence about my struggles with cocaine this past year, with my father over the past 34, and my apparent inability to live as others seem so effortlessly to do (at least most of them appear to do so less cerebrally or argumentatively than I). Then I have thought too much about these rather emotive, intimate things, and have, to date, written nothing. You and I barely know one another, I reason. Yet, I cannot shake the feeling that by corresponding with you, I will gain (and simultaneously become) a friend in word and "indeed," if you will pardon a rather weak pun.

Here is my best thinking on these three matters:

a.) I have never felt the compulsion and need for any person or thing with such desperation as I have for the baffling, more-pricey-than-pure-gold substance which is cocaine. Words are inadequate to express or explain the insatiable hunger this drug evokes. If ever I've wanted anything as much, it would be to find ecstasy in knowing God. I fear we, as a people, have forgotten how to enjoy the pure delight of communing with the Deity. I equate this thirst for God and this thirst for drugs as coming from the same barren place in the soul. It is a desire to transcend humanity, to find absolution and know joy, to "leap the surly bonds of earth and touch the face of God," to fly, unafraid of falling and never looking down. And though cocaine is a tangible, obtainable (albeit expensive as hell, literally) thing, it is too scary. Too scary and too destructive. It is impossible to sustain the ecstasy. It is a release so fleeting that if one blinks, one will surely miss it. I know I must leave the earthly pursuit of unearthly passions. It is, humbly and meekly, to God I must turn. This is, however, an intangible pursuit. Does one know when one has arrived at this place I so doggedly seek? Can one ever, truly, touch the face of God? One small concession: Next time I try to fly, I shall first obtain wings, one way or another.

b.) I have realized my father is a man. No more. No less. Somehow, when his ordination or calling to the ministry reached my consciousness, I expected him to be more. Either that, or I felt the cloth was not the optimum career path for our family. I could tolerate no hypocrisy and no spiritual weakness in him. He knew this, and, of course, could do little about his own humanity. We were both, I believe, often disappointed by this harsh reality.

As my own spiritual and physical realities have been turned inside out by my cocaine addiction and his personal quest to save my life when I could see no reason to do so, I have seen my father with new eyes. I have begun to know personally and therefore respect his tenacity, his faith, his courage, and his unflagging optimism. My father accepts life and its mysteries as they unfold. I confront and attack life, defying its unforeseen twists. My father knows peace. I want desperately to embrace it, but do not (as he does) inherently trust that it will remain or return. This leads me to my final point;

c.) I have a brash unwillingness to flow with the waters of life. A myopic salmon, I fight the current with every cell, trying to swim upstream, even if the journey kills me. Intellectually, I know and see that there are other, more restful ways to exist. Herein lies perhaps my greatest fear. Does one sell out on her soul to merely exist? How does one LIVE? I must have been absent from school the day and a half they taught us how to be grown ups. I get bored and then overcome by the tedium of adulthood: the tax returns and individual retirement accounts; the dry cleaning stubs and need to rotate the tires; the grocery lists and laundry lists and the film of dust that even now collects on the screen of my computer. Somehow as a wide-eyed child, I imagined that after I had passed the initiation rights of childhood, when I could vote and drive and drink legally, I would be admitted into the limitless realm of free choice.

Well, guess what? Real life is nothing like I wanted or expected it to be. Somebody has to carry out the garbage and find meaningful employment or surrender herself to someone who will. There is always a price. (i.e. I love my cats. I detest cat litter and the canned aroma of minced cat food. To enjoy the cats, however, I must tend to and care for them. Oh, and know more than I care to about their collective and individual digestive tracts. [Just as I typed this sentence, Henry David Thoreau jumped onto my lap and pressed his furry fat face into my neck. I guess I can forgive his earlier indiscreet travails with indigestion.])

Does this make sense anyplace beyond my own mind? Sometimes it just seems to me that life is one long, grand yawn (and I am using a kinder metaphor here than I otherwise might). I have simultaneously been irritated by, bored with, and afraid of missing some significant part of it -- life. I once told my father that it was backbreaking work being Judith Ann Hillard. (As I recall, he said it was no day at the beach being her father, either. But he was smiling, so I was never quite sure if I was more difficult to raise than were each of my siblings. I should ask him.) For a while, anyway, cocaine afforded me a reprieve from the assignment. Then it stole my health, my brain, my finances, my looks, my dignity, my goals, and eventually, my will and desire to live. I just can't recall how I used to do it. I cannot recapture the innocence, the anticipation, the rapture and sense of privilege I used to consider in being granted this, my life.

Yet, as I write, I realize that today I cleaned my new apartment and hung the remaining pictures on the walls. I filed my income taxes (with two days to spare) and am somehow receiving a refund. I purchased, prepared, and served dinner to my parents in my new kitchen. At 1:44 a.m. I baked cookies, and two are now cooling on a plate I have set before myself. Louisa May "All-Cat" is currently trying to rest on my writing arm. I see that I have written all night, as the sun is casting bright streaks through the blinds. Until tonight, the only occupation I found worth losing sleep over in the past many months has been cocaine. Today, I guess, I lived, without really thinking about it. Most days, however are not like this one. These are my thoughts.

Your turn,

Judith Ann

Chapter Sixteen - The Beginning of the Miracles:

"Accept me as I am so I may learn what I can become." (unknown)

"Lord, make me an instrument of thy peace. Where there is hatred, let me sow love; where there is despair; hope; where there is sadness, joy; where there is darkness, light. Oh divine Master, grant that I may not so much seek to be consoled, as to console; not so much to be loved, as to love. For it is in giving that we receive, it is in pardoning that we are pardoned, it is in dying that we are born again to eternal life." (St. Francis of Assisi)

Today Sally reminded me of something Eleanor (my former sponsor in AA who died of a stroke in her late-80s, having spent nearly 46 years sober) used to say, "Not even God can change the past." All I can do is hope to change the way I view the past. I am no longer sure if Eleanor was correct in this or not. I am not sure God views our lives in linear fashion either. I know there is a heavy, hard piece of dark wood that today hangs in my hallway. I carved out its words as a gift for my grandparents when I was 13, and after their deaths it somehow made its way back to me. It says, "God doesn't count our prayers. He weighs them." If that is true, and I have not the slightest clue where I heard or why I invented such a saying, then my prayers have been heavy on His mind for a long time. He certainly did a brilliant job of answering them.

Chapter Seventeen - Ruth's visit:

> *"Man is the only animal that blushes. Or needs*
> *to." (Mark Twain)*

> "These things I have spoken to you, that My joy
> may be in you, and that your joy may be made full.
> This is My commandment, that you love one
> another, just as I have loved you." (John 15:11-12)

23 April 1995

Dear Ruth,

Remember my favorite Emily Dickinson poem?

> *I had been hungry all the years*
> *My noon had come to dine,*
> *I trembling drew the table near*
> *And touched the Curious Wine*

That is how I feel, somehow, lost and almost dead but also
hungry and lonely and almost scared. I search for God but fear He
hears me not. I search for peace and instead, find cocaine. These
two yearnings are opposite but equal though cocaine is found here
on earth, or perhaps someplace beneath humanity. Sally calls it my
"visit to the underworld." Cocaine and its paraphernalia are
tangible things, obtainable (albeit expensive as hell, literally), but
reachable. It is the yin-yang, I believe. Heads and Tails make the
coin. Every city has a ghetto. The dark side of this craving exactly
parallels the light, which is the desire to experience God within.
As far below the surface of life as I have traveled identifies for me
the vast pinnacles to which I aspire. My need for this reason in life
is so huge I had to creep into the dregs of life to get my own inner
light jump-started. It's like this naughty two-year-old occupies the
addicted part of my brain and body. She had to get this bad to
attract my attention. She parks herself in front of the television

when the grown-up me is watching an important documentary. These competing forces are two identical sisters within my soul, both thirsting for enlightenment and actually needing one another. As much as I have needed cocaine, I have needed God more. Perpetually, I remain lost, seeking but not finding any peace.

I have worried that in telling you all of this, you would run and hide. And I knew I could not stand that. As close as we have been since the first day we moved into a dorm at ASU, I worried I would lose you too (alongside an enormous list of people and things I've already lost). I apologize for not trusting our enduring friendship enough. For not trusting God, whom I so longed to know, enough. I shall try never to repeat the same mistake. Do you know that I am nothing but terrified and maintaining an all-out sprint nearly 24 - 7? Every moment of every day and nearly every night, I live with my own jagged and tortured soul. Before my dad called and asked you to come to Phoenix to tell me goodbye, did you know any of this? Is the connection we share so powerful that somehow you knew? I wanted you to, and at the same time feared that you would see too much if I let you see me. And so I hid. I isolated myself and things got, not surprising, even worse (fast).

Please come to the desert to talk and walk with me. I need your guidance and friendship. I need to talk with you and remember how to be your friend. I need you to help me resurrect the person I have been in this, the second half of my life, so far, and discover who I am going to become. I am fighting something even bigger than cocaine addiction. I am fighting the distortions in my mind that have controlled my life in the past year. I am facing my limitations, my anger and shame, the reality of what I have inflicted upon my family and myself. "I grow old, I grow old...." T.S. Eliot wrote of J. Alfred Prufrock. But I, I do not grow wise. I know wise people. I am shown the way to the teachers, but I do not show them the small but central part of me (probably the two-year-old) who fears she is unloved and unlovable if she is not perfect. I have spent my life constructing faces with which to capture and entertain the students, the relatives, the friends, the people in charge. I have become a master of disguises. And now I am stripped of these costumes. I am naked, unprotected, and I am afraid. I have become unrecognizable to myself. I don't know what to do next. I don't know who I am. Why must I hurt myself so badly in order to learn what others seem so effortlessly to accept? Why can I not give up the struggle? Or else, why can't I just die? I've certainly challenged my spirit guides to keep me alive (maybe to prove to the unlovable part that they, at least, love me and therefore, will not let me die, no matter what I may do. In this self-destructive place, if I were to jump from an airplane, I would probably not pull the ripcord until my toes touched the treetops.

Please come to Arizona and help me learn to live again. Show me how. Help me clean my filthy apartment and equally filthy self. Maybe you can find a way to get me into a treatment center when neither my parents nor the staff at Good Sam could find a way. I cannot do this on my own. It is just too big and I, too small.

Somehow as a wide-eyed, overly observant child, I imagined that after I had finally grown up, I would be admitted into the limitless realm of free choice. I knew I would choose to sustain the anticipation I cherished every day of childhood Decembers. I would somehow opt to remain in the freshly-sharpened-pencils-and-new-notebook-hopefulness of late August rather than step into the collective-dullness-of-group-learning and disruptive-tardy-bell-doldrums of September. I was wrong.

The event itself (whatever it might be) was just never, for me, as marvelous as the moments leading up to it. I love the anticipation of Christmas morning far more than I do opening the presents. Wallace Stevens wrote in "Thirteen Ways of Looking at a Blackbird,"

> *I don't know which to prefer,*
> *the beauty of inflection*
> *or the beauty of innuendo.*
> *The blackbird whistling*
> *or just after.*

I would add to these only the perfect, tranquil stillness that lingers in the singular moment *before* the blackbird sings, when he is perched and ready and you listen for his voice.

I used to anticipate whatever was coming next in my life. I carried optimism like I was carried a Halliburton briefcase. Then I loaded that same briefcase with five or six loaded syringes carefully placed inside the leather loops. I shut the lid and spun the combination locks. Then I panicked that I'd loaded them upside down, and prayed I had not just shot them off as I'd shut the lid. I quickly spun the locks open to my combination to find that I had done just that: sprayed cocaine juice throughout the soft leather lining of my too-expensive briefcase. I tried to suck it up again, but it was hopeless. Another $400 or so down the drain. I go through money faster than I go through drugs.

One time in Philadelphia, when I finally started a load of laundry, I realized too late that my latest purchase of cocaine, folded inside a magazine page and shoved into the front pocket of my jeans, was just entering the spin cycle. The wet magazine page was still there, in the pocket, but the cocaine was long gone. Another $1000 literally down the drain. I thought these great tragedies at the time. They may have been the "accidents" that saved my life. Those may have been the very shots that would have killed me.

When I knew this was all the life I had left, I lost hope. My soul thirsts and I am starving.

It is so BIG to think about, but I have been amazed and humbled by the length and depth of our friendship. The places to which I have carried me, and therefore you, truly boggle the mind. I guess this is why I have been shoring up my strength (and reclaiming my vocabulary) in order to share each gory moment of it all with you.

I miss you, Ruth. I miss the time we have missed because I have not been healthy or present since the last time I saw you. I have grieved the loss of my students in a profound way. I have grieved the loss of so many of my friends. I guess I am mostly filled with regret. Regret and fear.

I am tired. I shall try to phone you soon, or you can call me. I hope you will come soon and help me find a way to return to my life. Help me remember who I was so I can find out who I now am. Please give my love to your parents; they have always been so good to me and I feel terrible that this is the only me that is left to honor their kindnesses. Feel free to share this letter with them if you can fit it in the trunk! Even for them, I just cannot pretend to be Ruth Poppins any longer.

I love you, my friend,

Judith Ann

Ruth did fly to Phoenix and stay with me in my dirty apartment. She awakened early and found some cleaner and rubber clubs and started in. It took hours for her to clean my apartment, but she sang and smiled as she did so, occasionally asking me (as I lay weakly on the sofa) if I needed anything. Then she began making phone calls. She told me we had an interview with a woman at a treatment center the next morning at 10:00. She got me up, got me into the shower, helped me dress, and propelled me out the door. They didn't have a bed available for four days, but she signed me up anyway. In her quiet way, Ruth changed and probably saved my life in just a few days.

She visited a year later when I was very, very pregnant. She watched me teach.
Today Ruth is a teacher of kindergartners. Never would I have the patience to undertake the tasks she masters. A few years later, after Olivia was born and I had moved into and restored an older home, she and her daughter Sarah visited and found me whole. Sometime after that, she and her husband Doug ran a marathon in Arizona and came to visit Olivia and me once again. Though years

may pass between our long talks or emails, our friendship has remained a constant in my life since I was seventeen years old. Ruth is one of my very own personal miracles. Maybe I am one of hers as well.

It's funny now, but at the time felt devastating. While she was cleaning, and I fell off to sleep (finally), Ruth propped open the door. As unused to the sounds of the vacuum as she was, I could not find Louisa when I awakened. Ruth couldn't find her either, and could not apologize to me often nor frequently enough. Dejected and so terribly sad, I sat at the top of my steps, outside, endlessly calling her name, "Weezer? Weezer? Please come home. Louisa May? Weezer? Where are you?" I called and called, to no avail. Now, Mr. Eliot had been going outside for years. Generally he brought back his latest bounty, something he'd stalked and caught and eventually killed. Sometimes a gecko, a squirrel, a mouse, one time to my abject horror, a snake (which Carmen had to come and return to a creek on a golf course near my apartment in the suburbs). I had been calling Louisa May for at least two hours that particular afternoon, alternately sobbing and resigning myself to having broken yet another promise. Finally, I called out, "Eliot? Can you help me find Weezer?"

"Meow," I heard, and he bounded up the outdoor stairs.

He had heard my voice calling Weezer for over two hours, but until I called HIS name, he remained a gentleman and did not intrude. (I found her later hiding in the closet of my den. She had never ventured outside; I should have known. Life with me, scrawny though it must have been was better than life outdoors by any reasonable cat standard.) Today I know that God waits for us in much the same way. As my pastor says quite often, "God is a gentleman. He will not force His way into our lives. He will wait for our invitation." Today I invite him in each morning and hand him the car keys. We have fewer accidents this way. Besides, who wants to open all her own doors?

Chapter Eighteen - Hortense Meets God:

"Give not from the top of your purse, but from the bottom of your heart." (unknown)

"For whatever is born of God overcomes the world; and this is the victory that has overcome the world - - our faith." (I John 5:4)

There were moments under the influence of cocaine when I did experience insights or moments of absolute brilliance. As I've mentioned before, mostly I just could never remember them. Sometimes, however, I wrote. This one-act play about Hortense, my nosy neighbor from the ghetto, is one example. I have just never figured out how to end it. Maybe one of you will know and write to me about it.

Today I am so pleased that I kept writing, even in the throws of ugliness and addiction. As I've mentioned, there were moments of clarity and even creativity (IF I wrote on the computer). This one-act play about my nosy neighbor and her "friends" in the ghetto is one of my favorite examples. I hope you will laugh and relate as you read it.

15 - 29 May, 1995

Prelude:

I think I should have been a spy, or a CIA agent, since I seem to enjoy hovering above the lip of danger. I could have carried a nickel-plated derringer in my inconspicuous attaché, worn a wire, carried my very own "I-Spy" pass, if I needed to get backstage at concerts and more quickly through sluggish check-out lines. I don't know how one actually becomes a spy, though, or where one goes to school to pursue this line of work. Just a thought. Speaking of spies, I've been thinking of the rumor circulating amongst my neighbors of the good minister throwing blows at Hortense, and somehow the mental picture I get always cheers me. I wouldn't be too concerned about him being a man of God and losing control like that. As I've considered the situation and his moral dilemma, I think I should mention, in his defense, that God himself may punch Hortense when she gets to the other side.

I have been giving "the other side" a great deal of thought lately, and my father **was** a minister (not to belabor my credentials), but I also resided two doors from our dear Mrs. Haynes for eight long months, and consider myself somewhat of an expert on this matter. See if you agree.

There won't be any technical reason for keeping Hortense out of heaven, of course. And she will, by the way, come prepared and eager to provide documentation of each Sunday service she and Jeannette attended, a summation of each prayer uttered by herself and Jeannette, whom she has molded and raised, and therefore takes personal credit for each of Jeannette's prayers and good deeds as well as her own, rather staggering, number. Oh, and in case it was ever needed, Hortense kept a careful record of the few good deeds she observed the neighbors doing, once in a great while, over the many years she devoted to paying careful attention. So, as I'm sure you will begin to see, even with God, "Hortense wears thin. After 37 years across the street from her, I can assure you, Hortense wears thin." (Source: LaBella "Lard" Somethingorother, Aug. 1994). This is the conversation I imagine them having.

Scene: Hortense is shown in to a comfortable, certainly not "goddy" office and seated before a distinguished looking man. "He resembles Bill Cosby, actually," Hortense thinks, "but he has Thurgood Marshall's forehead." She smiles demurely and glances at her watch.

WELCOME, HORTENSE.

Thank you. I'm happy to be here. Do you know when I get to see God, himself? Because I think I deserve to talk to God directly, you know, and not just one of the angels, or another one of those tour guides. Who are you, by the way? I didn't catch your name.

(Hortense waves her ledger books to punctuate her meaning and rearranges her expression so this man will think she is interested in what he says. She wishes they would get on with these meetings and introductions so she can go to her new house and see what is happening across the street.)

(God smiles benevolently, reminding himself to be patient with Hortense.)

I AM HE.

Who? You're not **GOD??!!?**

YES, I AM YOUR SPIRITUAL FATHER, HORTENSE. SOME SEE ME, SHALL WE SAY, DIFFERENTLY THAN YOU NOW SEE ME. AFTER SOME TIME HERE, I MAY BEGIN TO LOOK DIFFERENTLY EVEN TO YOU.

(Hortense wonders how she could have missed this. It is inconceivable to Hortense that not everyone sees events and people as she does. She realizes she is a more careful observer and doesn't hold it against others. "God is BLACK! Boy oh boy, she thinks, I can't wait to tell Lard about this. She'll just die!!" (Hortense will need to adjust her vernaculars a part of her learning experience.) In her zeal to spread the word, her hands clutch at her heart, as her fingers squeeze and twist the faded fabric of her housecoat (the one she likes, every weekday, to wear as she patrols the 2500 block of Grays Ferry) into protruding sweaty cones. It was just like that day Dr. James Milton came by Miss Judi's to meet all of us and they found out he was black. Angela had been at her weekly hair appointment that day, so she had missed it. Hortense had waited at Angela's front door, knowing she would be eager to hear of the good doctor's complexion. This was even richer. Maybe she would spend her free time right at the pearly gates so she could talk with the ladies from the block as they arrived, before they saw God for themselves. Suddenly she realizes she has not introduced herself and is a bit embarrassed, which is rare for her, by this clumsy oversight, but recovers nicely, she decides, by chatting amiably, to this BLACK MAN God.)

Mrs. Hortense Haynes. You can call me Hortense. I am pleased to know you. I didn't realize that YOU were God, youknowwhatImean? I mean, I had a hunch that you were someone **important**, like a judge or something. Do you have movie stars in heaven?

(She thinks but refrains herself, at great effort, from saying, "I didn't know you were BLACK!" Casually, God hears her thought and smiles. He saw **that** one coming. Lets just say it, I mean, a third grader could read Hortense's mind by watching her eyes dart around the room and God can hear prayers from several planets away. Ipso Facto.)

HAVE YOU BEEN SHOWN TO YOUR NEW ACCOMMODATIONS, HORTENSE?

No, the guide said she would take me over there when I'm finished with you.

("I'll bet," he thinks and grins again. At least she was kind of amusing, in an oblivious sort of way.)

YOU HAVE DONE WELL, HORTENSE. NOW IS YOUR CHANCE TO LEARN FROM YOUR MANY INTERESTING EXPERIENCES. I AM QUITE SURE THIS STAY IN HEAVEN WILL EXCEED YOUR EXPECTATIONS. DON'T HESITATE TO ASK, IF THERE IS ANYTHING YOU NEED.

Well, I would like to know which of the folks, from the neighborhood, you know? Grays Ferry...

I KNOW THE PLACE.

Well, I was wondering which of them I will find here and who will be joining us, youknowwhatImean? In heaven and all?

WHY, HORTENSE, THAT IS CONFIDENTIAL
INFORMATION. SURELY YOU WOULDN'T BE
INTERESTED IN PRIVATE FILES?

(God notices Hortense's mouth begin to quiver. He thinks he sees
one nostril actually leap with anticipation, as if it were growing to
take it all in, so to speak. Saliva gathers at the edges of her lips,
which she licks like a hungry puppy. How she would love just an
innocent peak at those records. She glances around to see it they
are kept in His office.)

YOU WILL GET TO KNOW THE FOLKS WHO ARE
ALREADY HERE. AND THOSE WHO HAVE NOT YET
PASSED, WELL, THEIR ETERNAL DESTINIES ARE NOT
DETERMINED UNTIL EACH OF THEIR EARTHLY LIVES
ARE COMPLETED. THERE IS ALWAYS TIME TO BE
SORRY, BELIEVE, AND NOT APOLOGIZE FOR IT.

I know what you mean. but you must have some IDEA of who's
getting in? What about Lard, across the street? And that foul-
mouthed Tiny, two doors down from her, who tended bar at John
and Bessie's Tavern? I never went in there myself, of course, but
everyone knew she worked there so she could drink while she
worked. What about that little white girl, Miss Judi? She used, I
believe I heard someone say cocaine, though I know nothing about
illegal substances myself. She was a teacher, you know, until she
lost her job. Her father was a minister, though, and her sister, a
missionary in Africa, so maybe there is some hope for her, in spite
of her sins. Oh, and that creep, Nate, who lived next door to her?
He drank, you know? He won't get in up here, will he? No, I'm
sure I don't have to worry about his sorry person draped across the
front steps up here.

(As is her custom, Hortense never waits for an answer to any of her
questions, and God doesn't immediately respond, so she continues.
God's eyes roll back in his head. He forces them down, but
needn't have bothered. Hortense does not notice his reaction, as
she never looks at anyone she talks to.)

Oh, the stories I could tell you. That Sherry, she was in *prison*! You know? And she shot at Nate when he got drunk. He was married to three women, you know? Of course, not all at the same time, though I wouldn't have put it past him. Well, *she drinks a bit* herself. I never drank, myself. I didn't like the taste. But I never blamed her. No, not me, I don't judge people. I just make note of what they do. That poor woman was desperate, living with old lamebrain Nate. He beats on that boy of hers, Trony, youknowwhatImean? Mr. Haynes and I never laid a hand on Jeannette, our daughter. I just never believed in hitting a child. Anyway, like I always said, that boy is getting big. He's gonna fight back one of these days and knock old loopy Nate on his, uh, youknowwhatImean?

YES, I AM FAMILIAR WITH WHAT HAPPENS ON EARTH. EVEN ON GRAYS FERRY, HORTENSE. IF I NEED A CONSULT ON ANY PARTICULAR CASE, HOWEVER, I KNOW YOU, HORTENSE, WILL BE WILLING TO SPEAK UP.

(Hortense is annoyed that God isn't interested in hearing her juicy and authentic accounts of what she witnessed personally on Grays Ferry, oh, and Montrose, but she relents on account of him being God and all, youknowwhatImean? Besides, it sounds like God is considering her as a member of the Eternal Judgment and Damnation Board. The guide had mentioned that one as she told Hortense involvement in the community was encouraged, and she should carefully think about her own personal growth, select an activity she would profit from personally. EJAD Board was the one, she didn't have to think it over. And what did that rather tall woman mean that I needed to work on myself? I'm in heaven, aren't I? She sits a little taller in the chair, eager to make a good impression as a fair and pious woman.)

This is heaven, right?

YES, HORTENSE. BUT I IMAGINE YOU WILL FIND IT DIFFERENT FROM THE MOST RECENT POPULAR HUMAN

THEORIES. HEAVEN IS A PLACE TO WHICH EACH SOUL RETURNS AT THE END OF EACH HUMAN LIFE. YOU ARE GIVEN A CHANCE IN THIS SOUL SPACE TO OVERCOME THE OBSTACLES YOU ENCOUNTERED ON EARTH.

(God sees that Hortense is not exactly riveted, so he pauses to see if she has any questions. This was not his idea of a fun afternoon.)

Yes, I do. Since you said to ask if I needed anything, could you tell me where I'll be staying for eternity? I mean, is it as nice as the home Mr. Haynes and I provided for Jeannette, you know, our daughter? Did I mention that she was our only child? She's a good girl, God love her. Oh, that's you. How funny.

(Hortense laughs at her own humor. She knows she's a quick wit. She hopes God notices, and wonders if she should point it out.)

I never thought of it that way. You do love her, don't you?

OF COURSE, I KNOW ALL ABOUT YOUR FINE DAUGHTER, HORTENSE. YOU COULDN'T KNOW THIS YET, BUT YOU WERE CHOSEN BY RACHEL, WIFE OF JACOB, SON OF ISAAC, GRANDSON OF ABRAHAM, WHO WAS UNABLE TO BEAR CHILDREN OF HER OWN. THEY TOLD ONLY A SMALL PART OF RACHEL'S LIFE WHEN THE PATRIARCHAL RELIGIOUS LEADERS EDITED THE OLD TESTAMENT. RACHEL IS OUR DIRECTOR OF CHILDREN AND PARENTING, AS SHE LEARNED IN HER LIFE ON EARTH, HOW GREAT WAS HER LOVE FOR CHILDREN.

(Hortense is dozing.)

RACHEL SELECTED YOU, HORTENSE....

(Her head whips forward, her attention again piqued.)

BECAUSE SHE FELT YOU HAVE THE ABILITY TO FOCUS UPON A GOAL AND NOT RELENT IN ITS PURSUIT, UNTIL

YOU HAVE OBTAINED IT. SHE KNEW YOUR LOVE FOR JEANNETTE, AND THE AMOUNT OF ATTENTION YOU GAVE HER, WOULD BE GREAT. ESPECIALLY AS YOUR DAUGHTER STRUGGLED WITH HER PROBLEMS IN BUILDING PERSONAL RELATIONSHIPS.

Jeannette had no problem making friends. She had plenty of friends. The other kids were just jealous of our relationship.

HORTENSE, JEANNETTE HAS NEVER EVEN HAD A BOYFRIEND. SHE HAS LIVED WITH YOU HER ENTIRE LIFE.

She is simply careful regarding, well, intimate relationships.

FURTHERMORE, SHE HAS NEVER EXPLORED THE POSSIBILITY THAT SHE DOES NOT WANT A HUSBAND.

Jeannette is not a homosexual! Who told you she had problems? I just detest people who spread vicious lies.

THIS IS ONE OF YOUR MOST CHALLENGING LESSONS, HORTENSE: TO SUSPEND JUDGMENT, NO MATTER HOW YOU FEEL INSIDE. YOU MUST CONTINUE IN YOUR STEADFAST SUPPORT OF JEANNETTE, WHATEVER SHE CHOOSES TO DO, NOW THAT YOU ARE GONE.

What's she going to do? I'll just slap that girl if I catch her being promiscuous, I swear I will.

SOON YOU WILL FIND ANSWERS TO YOUR MANY QUESTIONS.

Well, I just don't understand those people. Isn't AIDS a painful enough lesson for them to learn that what they do is wrong? It is immoral. No God-Fearing individual can condone such perversion.

THIS MAY BE ONE OF THE IDEAS YOU WILL BEGIN TO
CHANGE. I AM NOT A GOD WHO TEACHES BY FEAR.
BESIDES, THE AIDS LESSON WAS INTENDED FOR THE
HETEROSEXUAL PART OF SOCIETY. THEY MISSED IT
COMPLETELY, CLUCKING THEIR TONGUES AS THEIR
SONS AND BROTHERS AND FRIENDS TRAGICALLY
WASTED AWAY BEFORE THEIR VERY GUARDED EYES.
STILL, THEY DID NOT LEARN COMPASSION.

(Hortense had heard enough of this. There was nothing wrong
with her Jeannette. Why everyone knew that, and if they didn't,
Hortense would see to it they were told again. She changed the
subject.)

It is important to the Grays Ferry block that we stay together. We
are a close-knit neighborhood, you know?

HORTENSE, I DIDN'T THINK YOU **LIKED** ANY OF YOUR
NEIGHBORS.

Oh, I never intended to give you that impression. Those people are
very, well, important in my daily life. Not that you'll tell me if any
of them, like Lard, or Angela, or Mr. Wells....his nephew Jake,
he's a schizophrenic, you know? He burned that poor old man.
He couldn't hear worth beans either, Mr. Wells, I mean....well, if
they got in, youknowwhatImean? You see, I'd be interested in
watching, I mean, living near those same people again. I don't
really have any hobbies, and I can't play a note on the
piano......though Mr. Haynes and I saw to it that Jeannette, our
daughter, a dear girl and our only child, was provided with four
and a half years of private piano lessons and we saved for seven
years to buy her a piano. And we did it, too. We lived our whole
married life on the first floor and rented the upstairs bedrooms to
boarders so we could do right by that girl, youknowwhatImean?
We, Jeannette and I...she has lived with me her whole life. Lord, I
wonder how she'll do without me now that I'm, uh, here? We
didn't live in the whole house until 17 years ago, when Mr. Haynes
passed. He was a good provider, and left us with an adequate life
insurance policy. So, I had the house fixed up. Most people say it

is the finest one on the block. Jeannette was nearly 40 years old by then, and, you know, a girl needs her privacy. That's why I had it done, you know, for her. Yes, we let the boarders go and stretched ourselves into the whole place. It's a shame Mr. Haynes didn't live to have a bedroom of **his** own. But, you see, if he **had** lived, we couldn't have moved upstairs because we wouldn't have received that life insurance policy, youknowwhatImean? Anyway, is he here, Mr. Haynes, I mean?

YES, HORTENSE. HE HAS BEEN HERE SINCE 1986, EARTH TIME, I BELIEVE. HE IS QUITE AT HOME WITH US.

How is he? He was a fine man, youknowwhatImean? And a good father. He worshipped Jeannette, our daughter.

(Hortense catches her mistake just a beat too late.)

Well, he worshipped **you**, of course, God. We all did, naturally. We raised our daughter in a Christian home. Lord, that man was proud of his little girl. A better father **no one** ever had.

(OOPS, she'd done it again. God waits her out her, which is not that challenging. Hortense idles at a higher RPM than the new Porsche he'd been considering driving on the Skyobahn.)

Well, I am not saying that **you** were not a good father, youknowwhatImean? But Mr. Haynes was simply the purest man who ever walked the earth.

(Darn, Hortense wished she could think as fast as she could talk. God agrees.)

Not that I think **your** son wasn't pure, youknowwhatImean? Yes, your son was a kind man. Everyone loved him. Well, not **everyone**, I suppose, or they wouldn't have hung him on that dreadful cross. Well anyway, Jeannette sure loved her father. Will his mansion be anywhere near mine? Or will we have to share one? The man could grate on the nerves, you know, when he chewed meat and he did tend to stick his nose into other people's business.

REALLY? HE IS QUITE POPULAR HERE. CONSIDERED BY MANY TO BE SOMEWHAT OF A SAINT, ACTUALLY.

(This, Hortense hears. She is visibly rattled and somewhat offended. This time, she speaks her mind.)

A *Saint?* Oh, for heaven's sake! He may have been a good man, but he was no Saint. The man had his flaws though I did my best to remind and correct him. But he persisted, as if he hadn't even heard the words coming from my mouth. Oh, and people noticed, too. Why, one evening, after supper, while I was dusting the frame above one of the upstairs bedroom doors, I happened to hear some of the boarders talking amongst themselves. I was only trying to make sure we were adequately meeting the needs of our boarders, keeping a clean house and all, youknowwhatImean? I often wondered why they had that door shut, come to think of it. I would just have to go inside the room the next morning after all the men left for work, you know? Just to dust inside the doorframe? Anyhow, I heard two of the men talking, and one said, "Boy, I wonder what *his* problem is?" The man was referring to Mr. Haynes, of course. And the other man said, "That Hortense must have been a good looking bride." Naturally, I was flattered. I didn't know the men thought so highly of me, and I wasn't sure if I'd been beautiful, or just pretty, so I went straight to the box where I kept the photographs and dumped the entire thing on Mr. Haynes' bed, and found our wedding picture. I had to agree with them. It had been a rather simple wedding, so I had never displayed the one picture taken that day, but I had to admit I had looked smart in that ivory shirtwaist. But, just to be sure, I took the photograph downstairs and asked Mr. Haynes. He said, "You look fine, Hortense. Just fine." But he didn't actually open his eyes to look at the picture so I carried it with me outside and stood the steps, waiting. As the neighbors walked by, I flashed the picture in their faces and asked if they thought I looked pretty on my wedding day. To a one of them, the answer was simple and fast. They all said, "Yes, Hortense, you were pretty." Lard, you know, from across the street, even said, "You were then, and still are, a sight to behold." I liked Lard a little better that week. I have it here in my bag, if you'd like to see for yourself. I've carried it ever since that evening.

(Hortense digs in her bag without result for six or seven minutes, and then her hands drift away from the task, as if she's forgotten what she sent them in search of. God is rather relieved that he doesn't have to comment on her nuptial appearance. He sighs and notices he has been tapping the heal of his wing tip against the chair, so he stops. Instead, he examines the fingernails on both hands.)

Anyway, I'm not sure Mr. Haynes was all **that** popular, youknowwhatImean? You say he's here, hmm? Good. Good. What is my mansion like?

YOUR ACCOMMODATIONS WILL BE VERY COMFORTABLE.

("JESUS, BUT THIS WOMAN CAN TALK," he whispered via ESP to his son who shared an adjoining office, to his right. The Holy Ghost, who was rarely in, had an office to his left. Hortense is, as is her custom, waiting for the other person to take a breath, and only halfway, sometimes, sort of listening, youknowwhatImean? She is busy glancing over God's shoulder, out the window, to see if she knows anyone on the squash courts. She wishes he would move just three or four inches to the left. God hears her relentless banter, and holds his breath, wondering briefly if it is possible for her to hyperventilate in heaven.)

AS MY SON ONCE SAID, AND SOMEONE WAS CLEVER ENOUGH TO WRITE IT DOWN. I BELIEVE IT WAS THE MONK WHO DID THE XEROX COMMERCIALS. DO YOU REMEMBER HIM? YES, HE WAS CLEVER, ALL RIGHT. MADE A BUNDLE FOR THE ARCHDIOCESE ON THAT 30 SECOND STINT.

(He tries to divert her from her hawk's grip on this subject. It does not work. If she's anything, Hortense Haynes is steadfast. God is enjoying mimicking her conversational style, if not the conversation itself.)

ANYWAY, MY SON, WHO IS, INCIDENTALLY, **ALSO** AN ONLY CHILD, THOUGH, OF COURSE YOU ARE **ALL** MY CHILDREN, YOUKNOWWHATIMEAN? JESUS SAID, IN ONE OF HIS FINER SERMONS, I MIGHT ADD, "IN MY FATHER'S HOUSE ARE MANY MANSIONS." ONE HAS BEEN PREPARED FOR YOU, HORTENSE. I THINK YOU WILL FIND IT, OH, AT LEAST AS COMFORTABLE AS YOUR EARTHLY, GRAYS FERRY HOME.

Anyway, I'm not sure what the neighborhoods are like up here, but I want to register my request right now, up front, that I want a similar arrangement to what I had at Grays Ferry.

(God smiles but says nothing. Hortense is sure she is winning him over.)

Like I was saying, I don't have any hobbies to speak of. And I just don't know what I'd do with myself for all eternity if I didn't keep watch over my neighbors. Is Lard's daughter coming here? I hate to say it, but I hope not. That girl, Lacy, she has a terrible drug problem, you know.....well, not that I listened to what she said, in particular, but **everybody** heard her screaming at her mama in the middle of the night. And so disrespectful, she was. That child was loud enough to wake the dead, youknowwhatImean? Now that I think about it, I actually wouldn't mind a little peace and quiet.

(God loosens his tie. He makes a mental note to make an appearance tomorrow afternoon at the Vatican and ask John Paul if Jeremiah Haynes met the other requirements necessary to be listed among the saints. It was a miracle he hadn't shot her, or himself, in the head and arrived years sooner. And people thought he'd been hard on Job!)

As I was saying, I'd sure like to live near any of them who make it up here. But I **would** like my own mansion, of course, like the good book says. I often read it at night, you know? Kept one on my nightstand. And I always carry a pocket edition in my purse.

HORTENSE, I HAVE NOTED YOUR REQUEST. I WILL SPEAK TO THE PEOPLE IN MANSION DESIGN AND CONSTRUCTION. I LEAVE THE DETAILS TO THEM. I TRY NOT TO MICRO-MANAGE, AS A GENERAL PRINCIPLE OF GOOD MANAGEMENT.

(Hortense doesn't notice, but God is stalling. Instead, she is rifling through her handbag in search of her Bible. He had heard about living arrangements from the Gray's Ferry people for years, everything from a simple, "God, please make her shut up" to requests not altogether different from, though completely opposite of, Hortense's. The others specifically requested that their mansions be placed as far away from hers as was heavenly possible. Just that morning a group had rushed into his office, a few moments after Hortense breathed her last, and still somehow managed to call out, "Keep track of the neighbors for me, Jeannette. You can catch me up when you pass." Then, she died. God hadn't been sure if Jeannette's were tears of grief or utter relief. She had turned away to get a tissue from the night stand beside her mother's bed, blew dust off the Bible underneath the Kleenex box just before she blew her nose, and spotted Hortense's spare set of binoculars hanging by a worn strap from the corner of the top drawer. She glanced at her mother, whose eyes were fixed and open, as if she'd gone on to heaven ready to, as she said, be observant. Jeannette tossed the binoculars into the trashcan and said simply, "A three pointer." Unlike her mother, Jeannette did not look back.

{Hortense begins to gather her things, confident that her simple request will be met the moment she leaves. God extends his hand and for a moment, simply stares at it, as if he does not recognize it as his. He shakes his head to clear the thought that the hand may act on a will of its own and actually slap Hortense's nosy face

rather than simply squeezing her hand in a fatherly sort of way.
YES, HORTENSE WEARS THIN. AND SHE'S ONLY BEEN
HERE 37 MINUTES. He decided to check with the Pope about
Lard. Jeannette too.)

Chapter Nineteen - 62 Things Cocaine Robs You Of:

> *"Each one of us is somewhat like the liberty bell in that we don't know our true value until we have our first major crack."* *(Jerald Newman)*

> "God is our refuge and strength, a very present help in trouble. Therefore we will not fear, though the earth should change, and though the mountains slip into the heart of the sea." (Psalms 46:1-2)

I made this list while in the throws of total drug abuse. The handwriting starts out okay but deteriorates rapidly as the list continues. I remember thinking that I needed some Freudian "brilliance" in order to complete the list, and around number 43 my handwriting is almost completely illegible. I shot cocaine midway through.

Effects of IV Cocaine:

1. ears ring (or in case of accidental overdose, ears slam)
2. voice/throat feel "tinny"
3. heartbeat increases 25 to 125 to 225 beats per minute
4. hands, feet, nose, cheeks turn bright red (maybe it's the increase in blood pressure)
5. nose crusts and yet runs, simultaneously. Boogers form and show and you're not too inhibited to call them that (though I hate the word and what it describes) nor to dig mercilessly at them and then taste them to see if they contain cocaine. Generally speaking, they do.
6. armpits emit a strange, not-too-pleasant odor which no deodorant can defeat
7. you must shout, because your voice drops so low and soft no one can hear you, even when you repeat yourself five or six times
8. you are deprived of sleep for days on end (without end)

9. your teeth clench together until your jaws ache. This you barely notice (two of mine have broken in half, a front top one when I was trying to bend a sharp piece of metal so it would reach all the way into a glass vial that once held cocaine, and a back molar which was casted and then later pulled since it was so destroyed).

10. you hum constantly an irritating, monotonous tune (for me it was "Hooked on a Feeling, I'm high on believing that you're in love with me..." over and over again, not recognizing at the time the irony of that particular tune. Or I would hum hymns I'd known all my life ("All hail the power of Jesus' name, let angels fortress fall" though I knew they were not quite the correct words.) During the season it was "Have yourself a merry little Christmas. Let your heart be light." Just those two lines, endlessly, wrapping around themselves over and over again. All night. All morning. Always. The very worst was that obnoxious jingle on the TV Guide channel on cable (channel 75 in Philadelphia at the time).

11. a total inability to focus on anything necessary or worthwhile. An equal inability to stop doing pointless, profitless things (like crawling on the filthy wood floor for hours in search of a button you think you dropped. You might use only a flashlight to search, not wanting to "waste" time by standing up to turn on the overhead light). Ridiculous. I used to remind myself hourly to pull the clothes from the dryer – but two to three days would go by until the clean, dry clothes lay in a wrinkled, hopeless heap and needed to be washed all over again.

12. tiny spots and larger splatters of blood appear on blinds, walls, furniture, clothes, tabletops, etc...that were literally not visible just hours before. One doesn't even remember being in some of the rooms the trail indicates she was.

13. your vision blurs. Badly.

14. your movements are choppy and erratic. You trip often, on your feet and in your shoes. That is, when you get up off of your behind (Olivia calls mine the "gloomiest maximus" since it fell like an Austrian shade in folds numbering 46. 23 on each cheek when she saw what was left of me after

I'd been clean most of her life and then relapsed when she was nine. At my lowest of 95 pounds, she counted the rolls that had fallen from my back down below my skeletal behind.) or knees.

15. breathing is labored and difficult. Forget it entirely if you lie or fall flat on your back and can hear your thundering heartbeat. Or if you can't. Then you must consciously make yourself stay awake and count. Count to three to inhale, six to exhale. If you do this successfully, you will probably live. At least I did.

16. your handwriting grows completely illegible

17. no hunger or noticeable result of not eating (no weakness or stomach growls)

18. disruption of menstrual cycle (five months of no period at age 33, as I compiled this list)

19. mind obsesses around strange ideas that feel convincing and even probable. Mind
sets a stage which stars the needle which elicit a reaction, occasionally even a standing ovation, from the audience (the veins, or blood force, color, etc). This is a psychotic state, most likely, that feels like Oliver Stone accepting an Academy Award. The mind grows omnipotent and cocky, especially as veins are more quickly unearthed than usual.

20. fingernails grow thin and jagged. They rip easily and are perpetually stained with blood. Fingertips peel and stain even worse from the hydrogen peroxide used to remove the bloodstains. I felt like Lady MacBeth who could never again get her hands clean, "the blood, the blood."

21. paranoia sets in; especially when brain is writing and producing a blood play and calling for an encore performance. At these times the police follow more intently, the phone is tapped, the neighbors are plotting against you, etc. It is VERY hard to believe this is only paranoia, even later, when momentarily clean.

22. driving becomes almost impossible. Motor skills are impacted (pun not really intended, but apropos) and one cannot shake the fear of other drivers finding out there is a syringe stuck in your right calf. Distractions like the color

of red cars (arterial or veinal?), and the inability to judge distance all impair one's ability to drive.

23. a horribly stiff neck results from the failure to lift head from syringes, veins, bags, little jars, folded magazine pages, whatever…. For days and nights running like a large vein whose syringe has accidentally fallen out, but you don't notice until you are sitting on a warm, red puddle on your floral sofa.

24. inability to reason, plan, or execute anything except IV cocaine

25. cannot muster any feeling of pride or ownership in clothing, shoes, jewelry, household possessions, art that once one derived great pleasure in. In fact, one looks only for dark, old, loose clothing with no workable elastic as it impedes circulation.

26. almost every thought or action one takes involves the pursuit of yet more "cain."

27. sometimes one cannot get to the bathroom in time to answer nature's call. Nature hardly ever calls, though, but when it does and it finally reaches your consciousness, the urine has already reached your knees.

28. cocaine is a terrific and speedy laxative

29. your pupils dilate something fierce

30. sometimes you repeat yourself

31. your looks go, and they go far

32. you cannot read new material. You can, however, quote verbatim passages you read when you thought you were half asleep in college.

33. your finances nosedive even more rapidly than your looks

34. you do not care about anything but cocaine

35. you repeat yourself sometimes

36. showering, brushing teeth and hair require too much effort to dedicate time to on a daily basis

37. your skin darkens. This could, however, simply be the bloodstains you've not yet bathed off.

38. your clothes and laundry are perpetually stained with blood

39. you pour gallons of hydrogen peroxide on the real and imagined bloodstains on your clothing and sofa. It doesn't

take long for your sheets and shirts to fall apart as big holes emerge from the chemical bath they've taken.

40. peroxide becomes a staple in most rooms of your house (for first aid, needle cleansing, blood stain removal, and as a laundry additive)
41. you must resign yourself to a future wardrobe comprised entirely of long, thick, dark sleeves
42. your lips crack and burn and weird goopy stuff collects at the corners. It also collects at the juncture of your nose and eyes. Occasionally you notice this and do something about it. Usually not.
43. you sway and rock and quiver. It is not charming (as is Katherine Hepburn's palsy). At meals, when you attend, you sit almost parallel to the tabletop. People ask you, if you know any, "Why are you leaning?" You do not know.
44. Your veins invariably infiltrate, causing nurses not in the know to ask how long you've had severe arthritis. The swelling, impaired flexibility, and pain are that great (and apparently, that noticeable).
45. infection sets in, even when you are careful never to share needles (rigs, the druggies call them – and I didn't even know this when I joined their club)
46. you begin to call syringes "rigs"
47. you wait in cars (yours) for hours in the dark, in neighborhoods you would be too afraid to drive through in broad daylight
48. I'm told you can suffer strokes, heart attacks, respiratory failure, aneurisms, high blood pressure, psychosis, rage, even death. You think these will not happen to you. Not this time.
49. you age, but not wisely
50. sometimes, you die. Part of you fears this, especially when you cannot breathe without counting and making yourself, but are resigned to pursuing it fulltime none-the-less.
51. your sex life is entirely non-existent. So is your sex appeal.
52. your friends go away. They don't like you anymore and want the old you back. You can no longer remember nor find the old you.

53. even if you have advanced degrees in English, when and if you write, you will misuse pronouns, switching back and forth between first and third person (you, one, I)
54. you suck on the insides of your cheeks until they are raw and sore and bleeding; still, you cannot find a vein inside your mouth.
55. you lean WAY to the left (dominant side?)
56. you obsess over stupid, small things (pouring an entire bottle of peroxide on a floral sofa with red flowers because you cannot convince yourself it is not blood and you cannot wait until later, when your eyes refocus, to find out for sure)
57. you hallucinate. I saw a huge dead rat at the foot of my basement stairs. I even went outside for the first time in a few weeks and grabbed a homeless guy from the corner to come inside, past my "works" on the coffee table, and dispose of the dead rat. As dark as he was, I watched him pale as he walked through my previously lovely home and start down the basement stairs. When he got to the bottom, he picked up the stem and leaf of a dead plant and asked me, "Is this your rat?" I told him it used to be. He didn't stay long.
58. all things (going upstairs, bathing, buying groceries, calling people, any plans you make) become insurmountable obstacles. Life is overwhelming.
59. your hallucinations become more real than reality
60. you hear voices. Even on the telephone when it is sitting idly in its cradle. The people who call each other sometimes speak to you, but more often talk about you
61. you face death every time you shoot up. You refuse to speak to it. I had ten syringes prepared and lined up along the tub last night. It reminded me of *The Book of Questions* I had once played with a friend's family. The question given me was this, "If you had ten pistols spread out on a table before you and knew that only one of them was loaded, on the promise of a million dollars if you lived, would you put one of the guns to your head and pull the trigger?" Everyone before me didn't hesitate to say "no way" (of course, they came from a wealthy family. I did

not). I said yes. One sister stood and went into the kitchen. She returned with ten butter knives and had me close my eyes. It was near Christmastime and we were at one of their condos in Palm Springs. The sister had placed a strip of bright red tape on one of the butter knives. I opened my eyes and reached for the third knife from the left, holding it up for the room to see. Their eyes widened and someone said, "Bang, bang. You're dead." Sure enough, I flipped over all the knives and had randomly chosen the only one that was loaded. Last night in the tub, I shot off all ten.

62. I have written "U ave a bad w;lkrejwejpwerhe" and in the margin, later wrote, "Hey Jude, this is your brain on drugs." All these years later, I still don't know what number sixty-two is, but I'm sure it's not good. Maybe it says, "You have a bad reaction…" and then I must have, because right then I passed out. The list stops here.

Chapter Twenty - Valley Hope:

"Come dance with the west wind and touch on the mountaintop. Sail O'er the canyons and up to the stars. And reach for the heavens in hope for the future, and all that we can be. Not what we are."
(John Denver)

"(…you will be) strengthened with all power, according to His glorious might, for the attaining of all steadfastness and patience, joyously."
(Colossians 1:11)

Trudy Bischell, head nurse, quipped, "You'll be dead in five days, honey. I've seen a lot of drug addicts come and go through here. You are the worst woman addict I have ever seen." Trudy and I made a wager after I'd been admitted. She bet me I would not live to see the New Year, seven months later. I wagered that I would. The lunch tab hung in the balance. I don't think we ever had lunch together, but we did stay in touch. I called her specifically to say, "Happy New Year. I'm six months pregnant and as clean as the unborn child inside my body. I'm teaching and today I have more friends than I can keep up with." She was overjoyed then and a few months later when I brought Olivia Grace, the pinkest, chubbiest baby ever and pressed her into Trudy's arms. Years later she came to a spaghetti dinner at our church that a friend hosted for me to help defray the $1600 a month cost of my MS medicine. Trudy brought her daughter and hugged me so tight, I thought she'd broken one of my ribs. She was overjoyed and probably surprised to find that I was still clean, and despite the MS, incredibly healthy. So was Olivia, then six or seven.

Anyway, back to treatment. After Ruth left, I used as much as I could in my four-day-wait to go into treatment. I still had drugs the morning my sister Jaime and her friend and my father came to take me there. Cleverly, or so I thought at the time, I filled several toiletry items with cocaine and syringes. I unscrewed the bottom of my roll-up deodorant and roll-up stain stick for the laundry. Even if they searched me, I knew they wouldn't think to undo my plastic toothpaste bottle or the others in my cosmetic kit. As soon as they left me alone, I intended to finish using my stash. I think my dad and Jaime were astonished to find me packed and ready. Little did they know.

Chapter Twenty-One - More Miracles:

"Love is open arms. If you close your arms about love you will find that you are left hold only yourself." (Leo Buscaglia)

"O Lord my God, I cried to Thee for help, and Thou didst heal me." (Psalms 30:02)

By the time I checked into Valley Hope Treatment Center, I still had to have my wounds packed and repacked twice a day. They kept me in the detox unit for a few days. The first night, I was the only woman in detox so they had to pull a rollaway bed into a group counseling room. I was alone! Eagerly, I unscrewed the bottoms of my personal things (which they had not even bothered to search, to my pride's dismay), set them on a utilitarian chair with a purple upholstered pad on the back and seat. I had no sooner filled the fat syringe (probably 3 cc's) I intended to use, checked the window in the door to make sure no one was watching, shoved a towel over that thin window and rolled one beneath the crack in the bottom of the door so the night nurse would not notice I had turned on the light, when I turned to find that I had not secured a needle onto the syringe. Every drop of cocaine juice I owned had soaked into the seat of that chair. I tried to use the syringe to suck up the wet spot, not caring how many behinds had once occupied that chair. It just didn't work. I had once had a similar mistake on the bathroom floor in the Philadelphia airport. But that syringe had spilled on tile so I could find the wet puddles that were not exactly yellow (yuck) and pull them back into the syringe. This time it was futile. I did not want to be in treatment. At that moment all I wanted was to use. They had locked the door from the outside. Guess to which group therapy room I was assigned? Yep, that very room. It was not an easy task to tell my group not only what I had done and what one of them was undoubtedly sitting upon, but to turn over my stash of "works" to the staff. They applauded my honesty, but grounded my four-hour weekend pass to attend church with my family.

They assigned me to more meetings than the requisite three per day. I was on house arrest for ten days I believe.

A few days into my treatment an ambulance arrived and transported me to the local hospital. They were afraid I would not live if they did not first cure me of all infection. It felt like banishment at the time, but three friends from treatment sent me flowers and even came to visit. The chaplain also came when I called her in fear of my death. Jody refused to take a cab to Chandler, but a customer of hers whose name I can no longer recall posed as my boyfriend and visited me there several times. Little did I know that I would receive yet another miracle in the midst of the mess I had become.

Chapter Twenty-two - One Miracle, Helen, RN:

"Why is it that we rejoice at a birth and grieve at a funeral? Is it because we are not the person involved?" (Mark Twain)

"Our Father who art in heaven, Hallowed be Thy name. Thy kingdom come. Thy will be done on Earth as it is in Heaven." (Matthew 6:9-10)

I met another miracle in May of 1995. Her name is Helen Doss, R.N. She is miraculous for her professional demeanor, human insight, wisdom, and kindness. She is an exceptional woman as well as a credit to her profession.

I was a patient at Chandler Regional Hospital May 25 - June 10 of that year. During those 16 days, I met Helen when I was assigned L.P.N.s and needed R.N.-administered medications or treatments. These details alone may not be unusual, but the circumstances surrounding both my illness and attendant hospitalization are. I was admitted following a 4-day stay at Chandler Valley Hope where I had gone in search of recovery from a 19-month chronic addiction to cocaine. In the eight months prior to my admission, I had become an I.V. user, resulting in cellulitis, septicemia, and probably endocarditis. I had, by May, endured four skin grafts, one per limb, but had (upon my release from Good Samaritan Hospital) returned to using IV cocaine. Of course, I had just gotten sicker, and had found that the pain of injecting drugs was far less when I shot through the grafts. Of course, they quickly infected and further debreding and grafting would be required after the infection was resolved. A jugular line was administered for antibiotics and hydration, after 21 peripheral I.V. sites had failed. The recent history of my drug use was well known to my care-team, and was a major concern to my family, Valley Hope, and myself before and during my hospitalization.

Let me discuss one day, in particular, which I believe is representative of the treatment I received from Helen and evidence that God works miracles through the people who love and praise Him. On the first Saturday afternoon of June, Helen came into my room to flush the I.V. line and found me very frightened and weak. I had a temperature above 104 degrees, had not eaten in nearly a week, having spent the previous eight or nine days in room 229 taking delivery of and injecting cocaine into the I.V. tubing. Of course, I did not readily confess this to my caregivers, nor did any of them ask. Perhaps they were in denial, or simply unable/unwilling to help improve my situation. Then I met Helen Doss.

I was scheduled for surgery later that day and was terrified my heart would not survive the general anesthetic following a nearly continuous pulse rate of 200 to 220 induced by round-the-clock cocaine use. Without being overly dramatic, I can truthfully say that I waited, all that day, to die. Without accusing or judging my behavior or attitude, and I will grant you I was not an easy patient, Helen spoke to me with enormous kindness and patience while making it clear that she knew exactly where I was and what I was doing to myself. She was comforting and strong. I knew she knew, and was able, finally, to rest in the knowledge that she would not let them take me to surgery that day.

Helen asked if she could pray with me. I agreed. As she prayed to God in the name of Jesus to reach down and touch my burning body with healing and hope, I pressed my eyes together and tried to imagine that such a prayer could actually be answered. A few moments later I felt warm drops of water hitting my face. I opened my eyes to see the tears falling without check or embarrassment down the face of my nurse. She held tight to my hands and kept right on praying. As her tears washed my face, I felt the fever leave my body. It took much longer for the rest of me to heal, and I still had to have yet another surgery, but I had it days later when I was no longer on drugs and no longer filled with infection and fever.

Helen visited me in treatment. Years later when my grandfather suffered congestive heart failure and had been released from ICU to a regular room, the nurse assigned to him was Helen. Two years after that, it was Helen who treated my grandmother (in ANOTHER hospital) after she suffered a stroke and later died. She told me that she was often called to the bedside of the dying. She was able to bring comfort to the patients and the families and she knew that. She thought, praying over me, that she was helping prepare me for heaven. Perhaps she was; I just wasn't going there quite so soon.

At some point in this back-and-forth travail from hospital to apartment, from clean for a little while to using again, I realized I had to make an effort to explain all this to my family.

Chapter Twenty-three - Saying Good-bye:

> *"There is no end to what you can accomplish if you don't care who gets the credit." (Florence Luscomb)*

> "Do not be wise in your own eyes; fear the Lord and turn away from evil. It will be healing to your body, and refreshment to your bones." (Proverbs 3:7-8)

14 May 1995

Dear Family:

If I don't live long enough to awake from this nightmare, I want you to know that, up until this past year, I have enjoyed my life and each of you very much. My life, I mean, has not been enjoyable in many months. I still enjoyed all of you. Who could resist you? Remember how we used to talk about Jan being so sensitive (or, in Jaime's case, "sensible")? Well, although I kept it quiet, it was me whose heart broke over nearly everything from Jell-O and Kodak commercials to Dad tearing up each year as he reads "Yes, Virginia, there is a Santa Claus" when they reprint it in the newspaper. I won't even mention how the truly big deals affected me.

I guess that's why I had to escape (in a colorful variety of ways). That terribly sensitive escapist is the part of me that wrote songs and still writes poetry, stories, etc. Maybe I needed a desperate and tragic life in order to really tap into my creative spirit. When his life was falling apart, James Taylor wrote his best music. Maybe one has to suffer a broken heart in order to write a love song.

I love you, Dad, Mom, Jan, Billy, Philip, Jaime (hey, nice name), Mammy, Papa (also very nice and appropriate terms, as it turned out, for the two of you), Grandma Wilson (AKA "Pearl"), Grandpa, Ashton, Colton, Jordan, Ryan, [If you are reading this, I am sorry I did not get to see Africa and watch all of you grow up into the terrific people you already are and have yet to become], Lucy, Tinker bell, Giorgio, Niko, Roxy, Mr. T.S. Eliot, Nikki Giovanni, Henry David Thoreau, and, "like a shot," dearest to my soul, little Louisa May All-Cat, whom none of you have ever seen because she only comes out of hiding when I am the only human in the house. She makes my heart hurt every day when I think of her without me. Hers was also a tortured life before I won her affections. I hope one of you will take her and love her for the rest of her life in order to fulfill my promise to her.

Here goes, these are my wishes. Talk to Carmen about the cats. I'd like one or two to go with Jaime, one with Philip (our kids), one to Sally, Phoebe, Sarah, Sarah Benjamin (but her Daddy is allergic), Shelly, or maybe even Jadie Anne. But, if there are no takers, we always have good-old Carmen to fall back on. Besides, to distribute my most highly prized possessions in this manner, the cats I love to the people I love, would mean I'd have to adopt a dozen more cats, and I just don't have the energy. I wish I could stay alive for the remainder of Louisa May's life. But, once again, I just don't have the energy to continue living in this body my bottomless cocaine addiction has ravaged. She is my tiny and personal Clarence the Angel who let me save her so she could save me. And I've let her down. Just how many times can one life be saved? The difference is that George Bailey's tragedy **was** only a dream, and the whole thing was a movie. This is just too huge. I miss Shelly, Sarah, Ruth, Linda, Kimmie, Lauren, Scott, Eric, and all of my friends. I have to wonder if I wouldn't feel more at home and welcome in a new place. Complicity is a strange beast (GUILT). I wrote a will on this machine a couple of years ago. Do what you like with it. I have some pretty nice stuff -- you should wear it or hang it on your walls, or drive it (car AND golf clubs. Get it?), or pet it (hint, hint).

I feel I have truly ruined my life and I just don't know how to piece it back together. There are too many torn and shredded pieces, disjointed cuts, and not enough straight edges to form a border. I don't recognize me in the carcass that's left of my body. I have wrecked my perfectly useful and adequate body and scarred my overly useful (and adequate?) brain. It feels like things will never again be all right re: me for any of us. This is just too big. I crossed some invisible dividing line between *them and us.* Now I am a *them*, and try as I do, I just don't feel like an *us* anymore. I don't think you could unload me at one of your more profitable garage sales. I am tired. I am old. I have seen too much. I can't start this journey over again, and I can't pass backwards through it. But, I can move on to the next journey, though I will not willfully force this trip to its conclusion. But that's the only place left to go. Lets face it: I am not healthy. I am not robust. I don't think or feel well and I do not care. I do not even want to wave from afar to a physician. I am sure that I have inflicted some sort of brain damage on myself, and that, to me, is even more frightening than the condition of my arms and legs. I just can't live as a brain amputee. And don't even try to talk me into a prosthesis. I won't have it!! (See? Here's tangible proof that I am losing my mind.) I can't concentrate. I cannot sleep. I can't even type anymore. I feel clumsy and apathetic. I DETEST lukewarm and I have cooled to something hovering a few degrees below lukewarm. I don't want to go out in public. Dinner in a restaurant is almost more than I can handle. I can't chitchat or even be nice anymore. I can't people please, though I admit to never quite mastering that one even when I was healthy. I don't want to meet new people. If I don't already know you, it's too late for us to have lunch and catch up. I hate to shower or change clothes because the reminders of self-destruction are too graphic. If you doubt any of this, come take a look at my apartment. Even as I thought about Ruth's trip, I could not begin to ***make a list*** of what needed to be done, (and list making was genetically granted to us, wasn't it? I thought it was automatic, like peeing or swallowing, which are both showing signs of collapse also, but let me not digress any further), let alone actually ***doing*** any of it. You would not think one of your offspring (oh, except maybe Philip) could live in such clutter and dirt! (SMILE) I am a mess. So is my apartment. I can't pretend otherwise. It's hard enough to face people and be authentic, so why wrap my apartment in plastic perfection as if all I need is a thorough dusting? Who's convinced? I am not, convinced or convincing, anymore. I am trying to write a heartfelt letter to each of my friends across the country.... but my t y typing is no less apoplectic than my handwriting. If it flows well, I will finish writing the dissertation. But I do that for you, Dad, not for me. It feels so trivial and trifling to me now, when I am considering issues of life and death. Who cares anyway if freshmen girls are delighted with the cafeteria food and mattress depth in their first year of college? How did I ever think this was interesting stuff? I'd rather keep trying to write the exactly right poem, or learn to sing in perfect harmony.

With the typing... my mind knows where the M is, and so do my fingers, but my mind cannot get my fingers to cooperate. The right hand inevitably goes one key east of center. I spend half of my time backspacing. This makes me extremely frustrated, and then I get really cranky. It's like I've developed a sudden case of Tourette's Syndrome and have just blurted out something disgraceful, but I can't relate the voice to me, although everyone has turned to gawk and look offended. Maybe I am getting Tourette's. The only word that comes consistently to me as appropriate to what is happening that day or to describe how I feel throughout most moments...well, that four-letter word begins with the letter F (As I heard a softball player from church describe them years later, when discussing the language used by the opposing team, "They were dropping the f-bomb like commas"). This is how strained and angry and restless I feel at some point in every day.

This dreadful experience has, in a strange way, made me more real. I am like the *Velveteen Rabbit* whose fur was all loved off, only, in my case, the skin is gone. I just want to find peace and stop arguing with life. I long for that big, shiny, proud and tall Mama God to wrap me in her arms, hold me tight, and sing a lullaby to me. To whisper against my hair, "It's all right now, child.' Everything's gonna be all right now. You sleep now. Mama God will stay awake to watch over you. Sleep now, child.' Mama's here." And I will finally be able to sleep. [PS. Watch Carmen Lynn Pearson's video, *Mother Wove the Morning* and you will understand why a part of me can and must describe God in this way. After all, are we not ALL created in the image of God? Not just the men.]

To tell you the truth, I can muster up more energy for death than I can for life. You see, I REALLY LIVED! I didn't waste one nanosecond of it (with the truly huge exception of 1994 when I could do nothing else but waste away my life, literally and figuratively). I did almost everything I dreamed of doing, except I never went to Europe or Africa; I never skied a Black Diamond mountain INTENTIONALLY; I was never "discovered;" I didn't publish a best-seller (I am entrusting both of you, Mom and Dad, with that task.... Don't fail us all on this!); I never learned to play the saxophone; I never ran a marathon (You can do that, Philip -- sandwiched between everything else you do. I **know** if you set a marathon as a goal, it's as good as a done deal. The same will be true of everything **you** are determined about. You are our rock.); I didn't take care of you often enough, Jaime (I am thinking of the jeep accident when I did get to care for you -- I loved doing for you. Do you know this? You will be a wonderful nurse.); Grandparents, you made my childhood fun and meaningful. You have done the same for my adulthood. I always felt deeply loved by each one of you; Mom, you are beautiful. Oh, "you too, Dad." Seriously, Thank you. I guess we three helped each other to grow up. When I was a kid and you went away (unless we were at Grandma's or Mammy's), I didn't sleep hardly at all. The thought of losing you was so terrifying. I knew even then that you would have to outlive me, because I couldn't face life on this earth without you. I'm sorry, but you are stronger. You'll heal. I never would have. I'll just wait, in the next life, whence I am going, to reach out my hand, and touch the faces I love most. I don't know of any family who enjoys each other as much as ours. Maybe we are arrogant, as a group. Not alone, though. We know each other to be exceptionally funny, individually, and we laugh a lot. But no one laughs at the whole group of us; at least I hope they do not.

I love you all more than I can find adequate words to express. Ironic, isn't it, when it was me who said, "I aren't' doing nothing, Mommy, only just talking" since before I could walk. I try to be a wordsmith, but when faced with the stark reality that these may be the last words I ever say, out loud anyway, to you, the words have all left me.

You'll think of something to say to the friends I have had, and those very human and kind nurses who cared for me in Good Samaritan.

I don't regret not having kids. I would've been a cruddy mother, but I am excellent aunt material. You four made the last 4 and 6 and 3/4's, 8, and 9 1/2 years so much cozier. You sprung us all to life -- that wearing pajamas with rubber built-in feet and laying flat, with wonder and anticipation, innocence, under the Christmas tree just before bed on that magical night. You brought our family into a complete circle. You are all brilliant and beautiful.

Jan and Billy, you are good and kind and patient, if a bit rigid. If our childhood is the model for the one you are providing your children, they are having a great time. Take good care of them. I love you, Jan. You've been like a sister to me your whole life. I bet you're glad you don't have to do what I tell you anymore.

I want to be cremated. You can all decide what to do with the ashes. Just don't do as your friend's wife, and leave them in a cardboard box in front of the television. I'm not that fond of it, given the millions of other places my remains could rest. I don't want dorky pallbearers. Whose truly "pall" in those circumstances, anyway? (I'll lay odds Chase will volunteer his services to move the rest of me. Tell him NO. If I must be in a coffin, make sure it is cheap and made of pine or cedar, and keep the lid DOWN. And if my coffin must be carried, I want you to ask six guys named Paul, to pick me up. I don't really want people to stare at me when I can't, simultaneously, stare at them. It's eerie and off-balance. Besides, I don't look like me anymore, and I don't like the "new" look. Just don't bury me in the ground or behind a marble wall. Jan will explain the reason and the song that "grounded" this absolute requirement of mine since I was seven years old. Mountains, trees, ocean are more my style, having just acquired a very deep suntan. Maybe Billy could just drop me out of an airplane. You'll figure it out. Maybe storing me in the Taboo game box isn't such a bad idea.

Make your lives remarkable, all of you. Mine has been, even if the last chapter hasn't. I already miss you.

Your

Judith Ann

It was during this time that I also decided to write a letter to Patrick's parents. Remarkably, I still have a copy of that letter, though I never heard from any of them again.

February 21, 1995

Dear Mr. And Mrs. Ford*:

I want you to know what a three-month friendship with your son, Patrick, has cost me. So, I have decided to write. I have nothing more to lose.

The first time I met Patrick, he convinced me that since he was a doctor, I was perfectly safe allowing him to inject me with cocaine. Thus, our pattern began and very quickly deteriorated. Nightly cocaine use deprives one of sleep, often for days at a time. This effected both Patrick and me. He had already missed three consecutive weeks of work when I met him. I had just begun a new teaching assignment at the Prep school. I lost my job a few months later because I was not physically, emotionally, or mentally able to fulfill my responsibilities as a teacher.

I lost my freedom to live confidently. I am afraid of the threats your son actually spoke and the more sinister, silent ones that he left unsaid. I fear the craving for cocaine will return, causing me to lose still more. Physically, I have suffered with cellulitis in both my arms and legs, septicemia in the blood, and the ever-present threat of acute endocarditis of the heart, all of which Patrick, the physician, was aware.

I lost 18 pounds, dropping me into double digits on the scale. My appearance and ability to care for myself have both deteriorated. So have Patrick's. His nose bleeds and residue collects at the corners of his mouth continually. He drifts off to sleep mid-sentence or mid-meal, if he bothers to attempt one.

I lost my ability to make sound judgments about my life. For example, it was not a sound decision allowing your son to visit me at 3:00 AM (clutching his navy duffel filled with needles, syringes, alcohol swabs, saline bottles, sodium chloride bottles, and heart medicine he'd stolen from the hospital while on his rounds). Oddly enough, as it seems incongruent, he was insistent that we both ingest heart medicine prior to each cocaine injection.

In knowing your son, I fear I have lost me. Certainly, I will carry scars forever.

I just underwent the second in a series of operations to restore partial range-of-motion to both my arms and both legs. The next two to four operations will be skin grafts followed by plastic surgery in what is probably a vain attempt to disguise the horrific damage my body has suffered. The surgeon recently advised me not to look at my arms as he rewraps the bandages, which may give you an idea of the radical and lasting damage Patrick's methods of escape have cost me.

I have been ill and on antibiotics for the past three months. My parents, in desperation, flew me home to Arizona. They brought me directly from the airport to the emergency room. Surgery commenced the next day, along with endoscopic echocardiograms, EKGs, physical therapy, blood transfusions, and still more IV antibiotics. I nearly lost my left arm not to mention my life itself.

Though I am not blaming my *addiction* on Patrick, certainly the introduction of and access to IV cocaine and syringes, needles, and heroin fall squarely upon him. I should have recognized a problem in Patrick when, in treating a migraine headache, he severed a nerve in my foot. He had received narcotics from an AIDS patient when he told the man he would redistribute the drugs to other AIDS patients lacking insurance. Patrick shakes and trembles so badly, he missed the vein in my foot altogether. Oh, and I am not at AIDS patient.

Other red flags were his narcolepsy, manic depression, panic disorder, and chronic sinus infections. Patrick is adept at explaining away these maladies, most of which go unchecked and untreated, while he doggedly works at making drug connections and placing orders through medical and pharmaceutical supply companies (such as Schein, Inc.) while passing himself off as an HIV/AIDS clinic. Always Patrick is engaged in the pursuit of both legal and illegal drugs.

Patrick is severely impaired when he walks, drives, talks, and practices medicine. He is lonely and paranoid at all times. Patrick shared two prayers in the time I knew him. I heard scores of his prayers to St. Jude, the Patron Saint of Lost and Hopeless Causes, offered up as he routinely injected himself with too much cocaine and heroin too quickly, and then begged the tired Saint to spare his life. His other prayer was to find an addicted girlfriend. If he could not find one, he would attempt to create one. I trusted him as a friend and a physician, never imagining how quickly I too would become an IV drug addict. I hate him for this as he is completely self-absorbed and hedonistic.

I was initially impressed with Patrick's keen intellect, as I know you are. Yet, his self-destructive tendencies were equally as staggering, and unfortunately, those were contagious. I grieve the loss of the energetic, attractive, sensible young woman I was before this fall.

Patrick's employer has asked me to press criminal charges against him. This I have not yet done, and am not certain I will. I want this to be over in my life. I cannot forget, however, his methodical threat, "I will torture you slowly, and then I will kill you if my medical career is jeopardized." I have to believe he meant those words. Since I have lost so much already, why should I continue to protect him? I wish I had never met your son. Lastly, I hope you are able to step outside your own denial and reach him before he kills himself or someone else.

Sincerely,

Judith A. Hillard

* Full accountings of Patrick's arrest and subsequent release(s) from jail are recorded in *The Philadelphia Inquirer*

Chapter Twenty-four - Good-bye to the Queen:

> *"So long as we love, we serve. So long as we are loved by others, I would almost say we are indispensable; and no man is useless while he has a friend." (Robert Louis Stevenson)*

> "For He delivered us from the domain of darkness, and transferred us to the kingdom of His beloved Son." (Colossians 1:13)

My group gave me the assignment of literally burying the Homecoming Queen part of myself. We held a funeral, dug a hole, buried my tiara in the ground and threw handfuls of dirt upon it. I was assigned the writing of a last will and testament and somebody gave the eulogy. We all prayed that if the Ruth Poppins/Homecoming Queen part of me were given permission to die, the rest of me might live. I thought it was the most ridiculous ritual I'd ever attended. What dorks they were, the staff and some of the patients at Valley Hope. My teddy bear wore that tiara. Not me. I'd worn it only a few times, and those when I was 21-years-old and riding on floats in parades. They were not unhappy memories in my life. My group disagreed and gosh darn it, I wanted them to like me, broken as I was. I went along with it.

Here is my **Homecoming Queen's Last Will and Testament:**

Being of occasionally sound and seriously altered mind and body, I hereby record the following requests:

1. I bequeath this royal crown, given me the 11th day of November, Nineteen hundred and eighty-one, to the heavens from which I thought it came.

2. Since the idea of burial in the ground has never appealed to me (especially since I was in the second grade and, unfortunately, watched a scary movie on late-night television where everyone this little girl loved died, one after another, and she sat by the window and sang this song each time the hearse pulled into her driveway: "The worms crawl in, the worms crawl out. In your stomach and out your snout. Have you ever seen a hearse go by and think that someone was going to die? The worms crawl in, the worms crawl out. Playing pinochle on your snout."), I am requesting that this emblem marking the remains of my "queenly" days be entombed in the God Box, or held by the chaplain to be used by future patients of Valley Hope who need to feel regal or royal; those who need to be "Queen for the Day."

3. A photograph of my fifteen minutes of fame, promised to each of us by Andy Warhol, to be laid to rest beside my Homecoming Queen crown.

4. I also lay to rest the death letter I wrote to my family as I injected cocaine into my jugular I.V. in the hospital a few days after I was admitted into Chandler Valley Hope, fully expecting to die before I ever achieved even two days of sobriety. This letter should be cremated along with the image I had of myself both as hopeless junkie and conversely, Homecoming Queen.

5. It is my fervent and final wish that I can free myself of by burying the cumbersome and lonely labels I allowed those around me to dictate, and those I imposed upon myself, and live out the rest of my life simply being Judith Ann Hillard.

I am choosing, instead, to celebrate my life each day, for the rest of it, unencumbered by the expectations, either real or imagined, the world has of and for me. I no longer wish to be the queen. Today I have the chance to be a real person, not an image or ideal, but a woman, a daughter, a friend, a poet, a lover, a writer, a teacher, a contributor to the world in which I live.

Good-bye 1981 Arizona State University Homecoming Queen. Farewell intravenous drug abuser. Hello little girl who loves ice cream cones, finger paints, and soft puppies. Welcome to the rest of your life.

I have been given a marvelous gift, and like George Bailey, I have an Incredible and *Wonderful Life*. And though I have been and done many things for which I am ashamed, and others of which I have been proud, today marks the thirty-first day I have been granted by God to celebrate my life. Though I have lost my job, most of my friends, some of my family, my life savings, my homes, the good health I always took for granted, and much of my self-esteem, I am here today, having looked my own death in the eye and survived. I have buried quite a lot of the original life I was given and have been reborn. Today I have new and real friends, a clear conscience, a large helping of hope, and a fresh chance to recreate the rest of my life. Today I am clean and sober. Each day I grow stronger and more healthy. Today, though impoverished in many ways, I am a wealthy woman, and this is a richness no one can take away from me. Today my identity has been forged and hard-won.

Signed on this day, the 11th of July, Nineteen-hundred and ninety-five, by:

Judith Ann Hillard

Witnessed by:

All of the patients and staff of Chandler Valley Hope

Chapter Twenty-five - Eric:

> *"Love is a strange thing. It is a flower so delicate that a touch will bruise it and so strong that nothing can stop its growth. Think how often we miss love in a lifetime – by a wrong gesture, by an unspoken word, by not keeping silent at the right time. We lose it by the interference of others, by a lack of money, by a quarrel over a trifle, and yet we cannot live without it."* (unknown)

> "This I command you, that you love one another. If the world hates you, you know that it has hated Me before it hated you...When the Helper comes, whom I will send to you from the Father, *that is* the Spirit of Truth...He will bear witness of Me, and you *will* bear witness also, because you have been with me from the beginning." (John 15:17-18, and 26-27)

Though I was getting better, I had thrown parts of myself away at that point, knowing no one would ever find me attractive or worthy of human love again. Some weeks into treatment I prayed that prayer about giving me a reason to live. Here came the most athletic, most handsome man in the place, Eric, inviting me to go on a date with him for breakfast (you know, inside the facility). He laughed at all of my jokes as I began to heal and recover my sense of humor. I remember a sign-up sheet going around for whore's shoes. I handed it back to him and asked where we would find the stiletto heels in order to play and then corrected the spelling to horseshoes. I think God decided in that moment to let Eric help answer my prayer as he fell madly in love with me and the poetry I knew, verbatim. He did not believe in angels and had never encountered one personally. I knew several. So late one night, about ten minutes before lights out I held his had on the balcony and asked God to show us one of his angels right then and there. We asked my prayer in the name of Jesus Christ and with conviction absolute, I opened my eyes when he did and looked into the silvery, beaming face of a cherubic little girl sitting in the third branch up of a mesquite tree beside the parking lot. Eric saw her too, I could tell. But I made him say not one word, but rather both of us ran to get our journals and write down what we'd seen. We scratched away frantically and then traded journals. We both saw her, the angel in the tree: the perfect, plump little girl who beamed at us as if she'd known us all our lives. You'll read more about this particular answer to prayer in my chapter about even more miracles.

I made friends in treatment. Allen and his wife Michelle were in my family group. He was the recreation director who misspelled horseshoes and had become one of Eric's closest friends. Two weeks after Allen was released, he was shot execution style in south Phoenix. Michelle called to tell me the news. My friend LuAnne stayed clean and came in the middle of the night when Olivia was born to hold her and celebrate life with me. Our friend Carol, a nurse who had attended the same high school as me, but was a class below me and knew me only as the Student Body President while she captained the swim team, was also released several weeks before me. She hung her cup on the wall, hand-painted and hopeful of a life without morphine (she worked at a local hospice and had far too easy access to narcotics). Her life lasted less than a month. Her husband came home to find the dog going berserk in the backyard, and Carol's lifeless body floating in the pool. She was a champion swimmer and she drowned under the influence of a drug so powerful, she could not swim through it. The director of Valley Hope tied a black ribbon around each of their cups and hung them on the "wall of death." While I was a patient, two of my closest friends died of this disease. Today their stories join hundreds more in the "book of death" from which a designated patient reads one entry per night at chapel. It is a very sobering experience even when you don't know the creator of the death cup. It is almost unbearable when you do.

Chapter Twenty-six - Charmaine/Patrick Revisited:

"Life without friendship is like cereal without milk." (Maxwell Maltz)

"And they cried out to the Lord in their trouble; He saved them out of their distresses. He sent His word and healed them, and delivered them from their destructions." (Psalms 107:19 and 20)

My friends from Philadelphia called me some months after my return to Phoenix to report that Patrick and his girlfriend (a nurse) had been arrested and charged with first-degree murder! Though he claimed not to be the child's father, his girlfriend had given birth to a cocaine-addicted baby boy some time after they met. The child's name was Sigmund. You do the math. Anyway, frantically Patrick and Sigmund's mother drove the then-four-month-old child to the Emergency Room after they had noticed that he was not breathing. Sigmund was pronounced dead on arrival. After the autopsy and the mess the police found at Patrick's home it was reported that the baby had enough cocaine in his system to kill a 2500 pound horse. I honestly doubt that either Patrick or his girlfriend (whom I never knew) tried to kill the baby. I think they were probably just trying to quiet his cries. So one, or both, of them added cocaine to his bottle. Of course, the gal who "nannied" him was also a drug addict [Who else would work for Patrick, besides his mother who flew in from her mansion in Rhode Island every few months to clean his house, buy him food, balance his bank accounts, and launder his clothes?] so it was later speculated that she too had added cocaine to the formula. Patrick's family was wealthy and powerful. The charges went from first-degree murder, to second-degree, and then to manslaughter as I read about it in *The Philadelphia Inquirer*. When I tired of reading about him, he had been released from jail and no further charges had been filed. Patrick had been a doctor. Patrick had not been able to save baby Sigmund. Neither had his mother. Baby Sigmund died of a massive overdose of cocaine, administered not through a syringe as his namesake recommended, but through the soft comfort of a baby bottle. I pray he never knew what hit him. I pray he never suffered, but know for certain that for at least 13 months (or however long he spent in-utero in the body of an addict as well as the four he spent on this earth), he did. I wondered about Charmaine.

I tried to call Charmaine after I'd returned to Phoenix. Her roommate, a hair stylist as I recall, answered the phone. When I asked for Charmaine, she said in a rather flat voice, "May I ask who's calling?"

I told her I was Judith, an old friend of Charmaine's, though that was clearly stretching it. She was on my mind, however, and I wanted to know if what I'd heard about Patrick was, indeed, true.

Her roommate said that Charmaine didn't live there anymore. I asked if she had gone to Florida to spend the winter giving massages and the woman answered, still chilly toward me, "Charmaine is not in Florida."

Long-distance runner that I once was, I persevered, "Did she leave a forwarding number at least?"

"There is no phone number where Charmaine went."

"Is she in JAIL?" I asked, horrified at the thought.

"Jails have phones," the hairdresser explained.

"No, she's not dead is she?"

"I really can't talk with you about this," she said. "Please don't try and call again."

I didn't. I didn't have the number.

Chapter Twenty-seven - Teaching again:

"The people in one's life are like the pillars on one's porch you see life through. And sometimes they hold you up, and sometimes they lean on you, and sometimes it is just enough to know they're standing by." (Merle Shain)

"But if the Spirit of Him who raised Jesus from the dead dwells in you, He who raised Christ Jesus from the dead will also give life to your mortal bodies through His Spirit who indwells you." (Romans 8:11)

A few months later I had rejoined the world, secured a primo teaching job the day before school started that fall in my old alma mater district, and in the weeks that followed somehow remembered how to shop for food, feed myself, sleep at night, get up and get showered for work, and actually go there each day and just do my best. I think I weighed about 105 pounds by then. Eric was living with me in my apartment but kept quitting the construction jobs my mom kept lining up for him. I came home from the interview, knowing I had nailed the job, to find him reclining in his boxers on my sofa watching *Legends of the Fall* for the 3rd or 4th time on pay-per-view on my TV when he should have been at work. He thought of himself as Tristan, I guess. Anyway, as I unlocked the door and stepped inside he said, "Hey, where was you?" (He had missed much of the 7th grade due to a terrible skiing accident that cost him an eye and most of his grammar lessons.) I replied, "I weren't nowhere." He accepted that with a good-natured smile as he did most things. I then explained that I was going to get this job of nearly $50,000 a year as an English teacher and I was going to make friends with people I'd never be able to introduce him to without gritting my teeth over his misplaced tense and pronoun usage. He looked at me as if I had two heads, and I suppose I did. A month later he was long gone, back to the mountains and his parent's sofa, and I had just called a totally out-of-control student in my seventh hour class a prick. The night before I had purchased a home pregnancy test which was supposed to take three minutes to register a plus. Mine starting plussing the moment the urine touched it. I may not have had a period for a year and a half, but as Henry already knew, cradling my stomach with his soft paws each time I slept, I was pregnant.

Chapter Twenty-eight - Telling my Parents I was Pregnant:

"Let us go forth together to the Spring. Love must be this, if it be anything." *(Edna St. Vincent Millay)*

(If we honor God and live according to His word, he says,)…"so that your days and the days of your sons may be multiplied on the land which the Lord swore to your fathers to give them, as long as the heavens *remain* above the earth." (Deuteronomy 11:21)

Now as you might imagine, I have had to share some very troubling and personal details with my parents in the course of my illness and subsequent recoveries. But in all honestly, I can tell you that the most difficult thing I've ever had to tell them was on a Tuesday night, after a full day of teaching, having felt "off" for several weeks. I had stopped on the way home to purchase a home pregnancy kit. The directions told me how to work the test, as I've already mentioned. To my horror and ironically, to my utter delight, I found out what my heart already knew. Now my brain had positive evidence in the form of the plus sign which appeared simultaneously with the urine on the dipstick.

I knew I had to tell my parents first. I tried to sound casual as I phoned my mother. "Hi Mom. What are you doing?"

"Fixing dinner," I could hear her temperature audibly rising, "What's wrong?"

"Oh nothing. Where's dad?"

"He's on his way home from the office." Her internal thermometer was about to explode, "What's wrong?"

"Nothing Mom. Why do you just assume something is wrong?"

"Well, gee, let's think about why I might assume that. What *hasn't* been wrong for the past two years or so?" I think I could hear her begin some deep breathing exercises she'd evidently picked up somewhere along the road we'd traveled together.

"Can you put dinner on the back burner and come over here together when dad gets home?" I attempted to sound light, casual, friendly.

"Ummh, yes. We can." She was not buying my good neighbor visit. "Is something wrong, Jude?"

I could not lie to her, nor could I just blurt this particular bomb over the telephone. "Just come over."

When I saw them pull up into the parking lot of my second story apartment, my mother nearly sprinting to my door, I had a moment of panic. I had not rehearsed a speech, ever, of this magnitude. I had, however, already prepared a platter of various yuppie crackers arranged around a cheese ball. Hurriedly, I grabbed the test and stuck it beneath the bottom lip of the sofa and simultaneously spotting a lottery ticket on the front of my fridge, impulsively set it beneath the cheese ball. They practically pushed me over in their haste to get inside and figure things out. "What's going on?" my mother demanded.

"Have a cracker and some cheese," I suggested.

"Something is wrong. I just knew it," she announced.

I quietly mentioned that she should look beneath the cheese ball. She lifted it and cocked her head at the lottery ticket laying there. Recognition dawned on her face and she said very slowly, "You've won the lottery?"

"I don't know," I said happily. "But "you can't win if you don't play" (quoting a long-term Arizona Lotto advertising jingle).

"Okay already, why did you call us over?" Irritation is growing, concern is abating. This is still the voice of my mother, if you can't hear that in your own mind.

I walked to my sofa, reached under it, and retrieved the plastic tube. My mother shrieked and shielded her eyes. "What is that?" Concern returned. Make that panic. "What IS that thing?" I guess she feared I'd produced or found another syringe as that was one of my hiding places, along with the huge arrangement of silk plants I had in a tin bucket, inside a large c.d. case, behind the fake backs of a few dresser drawers, in the bottom of full tissue boxes, etc.

My father caught on much more quickly. "I think she's trying to tell us something, Gin."

"Well, what is it? What is she not saying? And why doesn't she just say it?"

"I think our daughter is pregnant," he could see the big red plus sign himself as he gingerly held the gizmo.

"She's WHAT?"

"Yes mom, I'm pregnant. But "I don't know nothin' 'bout birthin' no babies," I declared, truer words never spoken.

My father asked, "Have you considered your options? I mean, you're barely back on your feet, among the living. Will you offer this baby up for adoption?"

I honestly had not thought about it, but unfamiliar maternal feelings hammered in my bloodstream and they must have been generational, as my mother practically collapsed into a chair in my dining room and said, "Wait a minute here. I won't have strangers raising MY grandchild."

I told them there, at my table, about my cry of desperation to God to give me a reason to live. It was my feeling that this was perhaps the answer to that prayer. Remember dear reader, I told you that God has a measurable and abundant sense of humor.

Chapter Twenty-nine - Owning up:

"Raising a family seems to be one of those tasks, like losing weight or waxing the car, that is less fun to be doing than to have done." (Campbell)

"For I will restore you to health and I will heal you of your wounds, declares the Lord..." (Jeremiah 30:17)

I remember asking the 6 foot, 5 inch linebacker of a principal if I could speak to him after school one day soon after I'd told my family my news. He amicably agreed (thinking me quite a find with my Ivy League education and years of teaching experience) and met me in the hallway outside my classroom. I explained that he was going to have to fire me.

"WHY?" he asked, eyes huge in disbelief.

I explained that I had called an out-of-control ADHD kid a bad name in front of his entire class in order to regain control of the room, which he had adeptly usurped.

"What did you call him?" my boss inquired. I thought about lying and saying I'd called him a "prig" and the kids had just misunderstood, therein securing my position. Then I remembered the fact that I was single and pregnant and new to the place, having almost lost everything awfully recently, so I just told him the truth.

"Who was the kid?" was his next question.

I told him and he laughed with his head tossed back.

"He IS a prick. His mother knows that. She won't call."

Okay. The truth works out sometimes; I pressed on. "I'm pregnant," I stated, as flat-footed as I'd ever said anything.

He looked at me and cocked his head, much as Henry had done when I'd announced, "Oh Henry, we're pregnant. I don't know nothing bout birthin' no babies." My principal put his huge arms around my shoulders and said, "I think congratulations are in order, not a pink slip."

"But," I protested, "I'm single."

"I'm aware of that," he explained. "You'll need us even more than you would if you were married."

As I hit my knees that night, I had to laugh at the sense of humor God showed in answering my prayer. You see, I had learned in treatment that 96% of cocaine addicts will not stay clean more than six months. Of those who do, 96% will not make it to the two-year mark. The two-year mark is critical as it takes that long to restore the dopamine and endorphins, or whatever it is, that one's brain needs in order to feel good. Cocaine depletes the natural ability to feel good. In fact, I used to say and actually believe that I'd been saved so I could spend the rest of my life changing the cat litter and rotating the tires on the car. And that might have been true had God not chosen the brilliant answer he did to my prayer. I might have forgotten to feed me again, I might have hurt myself once more, but I would NEVER damage that unborn child inside me.

Thinking of these small and humongous miracles, I decided driving to school one morning that regular people get their happiness in little doses all day long. Someone waves them into traffic, a stranger lets them ahead in the grocery line if they have only a few items, they get hugged, they catch the lights all green. Little increments of life ease in throughout the day. A cocaine addict gets all 24-hours worth of happiness in the first eight seconds. Then that is it. She spends the rest of the 23 hours, 59 minutes and 52 seconds trying to repeat it. It never works; but she forgets that from the day before and chases it all day, all night, all week maybe.

Chapter Thirty - The Pregnancy:

"Every act of kindness is a little bit of love we leave behind. Every summer sun that has passed our way serves to light every day ... so when we have gone what we do lives on, you know. Every act of kindness is a little bit of love we leave behind."
(Paul Williams and Kenny Ascher)

"Behold, I will bring to it health and healing, and I will heal them; and I will reveal to them an abundance of peace and truth." (Jeremiah 33:6)

As a high-risk pregnancy, with our very close family friend as my ob/gyn, I had random drug screens and ultra sounds every month of my pregnancy. The night she was born, I had 10 months of clean time behind me. I nursed my child another 15 months just to be safe. Two years and one month later, I nursed her for the last time free of fear, free of addiction, knowing that she needed me to be present as her parent and that left no room for further at-home medical/chemical experimentation. I knew her middle name would be Grace the moment it was confirmed that my child was a girl (I already knew that in my heart). Grace: God's gift we do not deserve but we get anyway. Perfect, pure love. That is Grace. I was granted Grace through no particular talent or genius IQ or accomplishment on my part. It was given to me as a "brown-paper package, tied up with string," simply because I had begged for a reason to live. Brilliant but maybe myopic on the part of God who could, by the way, clearly still hear me.

Less than six weeks after learning my shocking news, my parents helped me qualify for, repaint, clean every inch of, and move into a home about a mile from theirs. My mother started searching for the perfect crib and rocking chair for me. They took turns accompanying me to Lamaze classes, along with my sister Jaime who was after that semester living with me in the guest room, taking a break from college in northern Arizona.

Jaime and I started two lists, which we kept on the refrigerator. Once we knew she was a girl, we wrote a LONG list of girl names we just could not abide and a much shorter list of girl names we liked. I knew almost immediately that her middle name would be Grace. I knew she was a gift from God which I had done nothing to deserve, but was being given anyway. I knew she was the angel girl Eric and I had seen in the desert tree. I knew she was my greatest miracle yet.

My parents both told me they had never seen a happier pregnant woman in their lives. All of the doldrums of those first two years of recovery from cocaine addiction were simply gone, replaced with the love and hope and joy of robust health and a brand new baby. I just never knew I wanted one until I was having one. I sat at the piano I grew up playing, which my parents had transplanted to my living room (after I had one) every afternoon and played and sang songs for my baby. I could feel her dancing along inside my body. I reveled in each kick, each hiccup, each movement of my daughter.

At about six weeks into the pregnancy, I suffered a terrible jolt of pain and had to slide, sweating, down the front wall of my classroom as the last group of students tumbled out at the bell. Immediately, I noticed that I was hemorrhaging as well. I pounded on the wall I shared with another teacher, the mother of two young children, who came in and assessed the situation immediately. She told me to sit perfectly still and she would get help. Terrified that my fellow teachers would see my skin grafts if paramedics arrived, I explained that I just needed to get to my mother who was taking me to the neonatal specialist that afternoon anyway. The department secretary drove me to my parent's house and we went immediately to Marlin's office. They did an ultrasound and determined that the placenta was separating from the uterine wall, hence the bleeding.

Marlin instructed me to go home with my parents and lie flat for five days. I was not to teach, not to walk, not even to the bathroom. Rather, my father was to carry me there. Mom hurriedly made a bed for me on their sofa, close to the hall bath and there I remained, prayerful, for the full five days. Weeping, I told my parents, "I just cannot lose this child. This child needs to be born." They both agreed. You see, she was a miracle in that I might well have fallen into depression or discouragement in those first six and then 24 months and hurt myself. But I would NEVER have hurt my baby. She was all innocence and purity, perfectly and wonderfully made.

Chapter Thirty-one - Friends Again:

*"For faith is a force that is greater than knowledge
of power or skill. And many defeats turn to
triumph, if you trust in God's wisdom and will. For
faith is a mover of mountains – there's nothing that
God cannot do. So start out today, with faith in
your heart, and climb 'til your dream comes true."
(Helen S. Rice)*

"Again I say to you, that if two of you agree on
earth about anything that they may ask, it will be
done for them by My Father who is in heaven."
(Matthew 18:19)

Friends came into my life like sunshine that year I returned
to rejoin the living. Craig and Stacey, Toby, Marsha, Connie,
Anne, Miriam, Evan and Patti, Don and Leti, Ruth R., Ruth L.,
Ginny, Sandy, Patti, and scores of others (mostly those with whom
I taught). Even my students felt extra attuned that year (or maybe
it was me, more tuned in to them than I had been to the previous
generation of students I had taught). They seemed to know, even
before I ever opened up and told anyone, that I had survived the
sinking of the Titanic; that I was a walking miracle. When they
learned I was pregnant, their love for me only deepened.

I remember a surprise baby shower my seniors threw for
me one afternoon. I had them all write me advice about child
rearing that they wished their parents had known. I have them still
and will someday write them into a sequel of this tale. They are
delightful, outrageous, and adorable. They had ordered a cake for
me, had decorated the classroom over their lunch hour, had chosen,
purchased, and carefully wrapped gifts, and were bubbling over
with excitement at being able to give something back to me. I
remain, to this day, so very touched and humbled by the kindness
of young people. If we treat them like children, as do too many
teachers, they respond in kind. Feeling so fortunate to be with
them that year, as I grew progressively larger (have I mentioned

yet that I gained 71 pounds during my pregnancy, so I know of what I speak), I was real with them. I had no guises or pretenses. I shared the real me with them, and to my surprise and delight, they loved me even more than the years of students who proceeded them for whom I had tried so hard to be perfect.

My department (over 22 English teachers alone) also threw a surprise baby shower for us, inviting my parents and a few friends from other departments. It was held at the home of my department chair, Connie, who truly knows how to throw a party. I remember seeing the cake, the bassinet, the car seat, the swing, the bouncy seat, and scores of other baby things and letting the tears run unchecked down my face. My parents leaned into me, concerned to find me upset. But these were not tears of pain or grief or loss. These were tears of joy. I told my parents, "Look at my life today. Wonderful, generous friends and their families surround me and they are here because they genuinely care for my baby and me. Look at my life one year ago. I didn't have any friends left. I'd used them all up and discarded them like forever-blunted needles. I can't believe God is being so kind to me through so many good people." I know my parents shared, if not in my tears, at least in my joy. It really was infectious.

Chapter Thirty-two - The Arrival of Our Miracle:

"I am so glad you and I are here to see and hear and be. And I am more than glad that you are you. How lonely I would be if you were not..." (Kahlil Gibran)

"He who did not spare His own Son, but delivered Him up for us all, how will He not also with Him also freely give us all things?" (Romans 8:32)

Jaime was scheduled to be my "coach" though it was determined ahead of time that I would have a caesarian section. The baby's head was stuck in my pelvis, trapped up against the left pelvic bone (driver side). I had not felt her move in the last two weeks and was growing more and more uncomfortable with her quietude. I taught on Friday, April 20th, 1996 and remember a boy asking me first period that day if he should boil water. I laughed and asked him what we would do with it? He did not know, of course, nor did I. And as I've mentioned before, we were not in the old Wild West. Jaime went to Rocky Point, Mexico that weekend with her friends. My C-section was scheduled for Tuesday morning, April 23rd. I felt as if she should stay, but she said she would be back well ahead of time for the birth of our baby girl.

Mom and I went garage-saling the next morning and afternoon. It was very hot and I remember asking one woman if I could sit in a wooden chair she was selling (for four dollars). She said yes and also let me use her restroom and brought me a glass of ice water. She said her name was Vicky and asked where I was going to deliver my baby. I asked, "How about right here on your driveway?"

"Fine by me," she quipped. "I'm a neonatal nurse."

We quickly discovered that though she only worked weekends, she did work at Desert Samaritan where I was scheduled to have my child and she loved my doctor, assuring us that he was the very best in the business. I bought her chair and off we went.

Later that day, Mom and I shared a late lunch at Ed Debevek's (a 50s-style diner I miss almost every week since it closed). We ordered a meatloaf sandwich on sourdough and split it, and we each had a chocolate soda made with vanilla ice cream (of course). After we drove back to Tempe, I felt odd. I did not feel pain; just uneasy and restless. My parents asked if I was in labor.

I responded, "How should I know?" We drove to triage at the hospital. They checked my heart rate and the baby's, determined I was not in labor and we were both doing very well. They did phone Marlin who spoke to me over the phone from the restaurant where one of his partners and their wives were dining. He asked me why I had come to triage and I answered him, truthfully, "I just had a creepy feeling and thought we should get this baby out now." He sent me home, telling me not to worry and that he would see us Tuesday morning. We went ahead and toured the facility while we were there and were almost to the car when a nurse came running after us. "Ms. Hillard, Ms. Hillard. Your doctor is on the phone again and he wants to talk to you."

We went back inside and Marlin said, "I just spoke to Sheri (his wife) and my partner, and well, I have a creepy feeling too. Let's get this baby born tonight. I'll meet you there in a half an hour."

I raced through my house so that I could shower the day and garage sales off of me, not sure how many days it would be before I'd get another shower. My hospital bag was ready to go, except for the popsicles and fresh fruit. I also grabbed a book called *You Are Your Birthday* and was trying to determine if I liked the personality better on April 20th or 21st.

It was 11 PM by the time we returned to the hospital. Even if I had been speedier, Henry (my cat) ran out the door when my father opened it and it took about 20 minutes for dad to find him and bring him home. Marlin was not pleased with us when we arrived. I had pretty well decided to drag my feet as much as possible so that my child would be born on the 21st, as was I, and on a Sunday, as was I in the other month that starts with the letter A. The 21st promised me an outgoing, charming, friendly, talkative personality. [Boy, was it right. I can remember when Olivia didn't walk; I cannot remember when she didn't talk, and she has never stopped in over ten years at the time of this writing.]

I dilly-dallied while the nurse was waiting to start my IV. Marlin asked me which of my parents I wanted to accompany me in the operating room. I said I wanted them both. He shook his blue-covered head and refused, explaining that it was a sterile field, an operating room, and there could be only one other person in the room.

"Very well," I said. "Then you choose."

He looked back and forth between my parents whom he knew and loved. He knew the agony they had both endured with me and realized that this blessing of not just my life, but the life of another, were paramount to our family's hope and unity. Somewhat resignedly, he shook his defeated head and smiled. "Okay, you can both come in. But you do exactly as I say and stay out of the way with that video camera."

I asked the anesthesiologist a million questions, not just to stall for midnight (it was about a quarter 'til at that point), but because I was disappointed that the only Lamaze technique I would get to use would be the breathing exercises I'd practiced while he inserted a very long needle into my spine in order to give me a full spinal block. I was nervous about this and asked where Marlin was. The very cocky doctor answered that until HE gave the nod, he was the Skipper.

My father laughed as he recorded my comeback. "And after Marlin comes in, who are you? Gilligan?"

I needn't have dawdled. Once I was numbed and catheterized (Thank heaven they numbed me first) and my enormous belly was cleaned with iodine and prepped (I'll spare you the grosser details), they finally made their incision across my medicine ball stomach and tried to free the baby. She started screaming and I kept asking my mother, seated at my head, what she looked like.

My mom said, "I can't see her. She's not out yet." We should have known then that we were birthing a talker. She squawked the entire 6 ½ minutes it took both doctors to dislodge her head. They try to have the baby out in under one minute. Our baby was so large in my narrow pelvis that Marlin looked over the curtain at me once and announced that they might have to break my pelvic bone to get her out. I told him to break every bone in my body if they had to; just save my child. He nodded, sweating, and went back to work.

I later learned that my father had gotten seasick taping the delivery. It was not the cutting or the blood that disturbed him. It was the sight of two large men leaning all of their weight against the soft head of that infant and my bones. "Gilligan" ran from me and helped my father (and the camera) slide to the floor before he fell. We have a recording of several minutes of floor tile, but can still hear the rolling conversations in the room.

Me: "Is she out yet?"

Mom: "Not yet."

Me: "Is she okay?"

A nurse: "She's screaming, that's a good sign."

Me, panicky: "I can't breathe," and the anesthesiologist explained that he just may have, perhaps, inadvertently placed the spinal block a tidge too high, therein paralyzing the feeling in my ribcage and lungs.

He asked me, "You're talking, aren't you?"

"Yes," I answered.

"Then you're breathing. Besides, if you stop, I have all this equipment here to breathe for you (how reassuring). And once the baby's out, I'm going to put a marguerita in your line and you won't care."

Just then, at 12:15 on Sunday the 21st of April, 1996, I saw the doctors hand a very purple, angry baby to the team of waiting nurses who cleaned her up, sucked out her nose and mouth, put a pink ski cap on her head and wrapped her in a striped, soft flannel blanket. Someone brought her over to my head and I touched her gorgeous fat face.

I could hear my father saying, "She's a keeper. Just look at her. She must weigh ten pounds."

I told my mother, she doesn't look like a Victoria Grace (the name I had settled upon at last). My mom agreed. "I can only think of Grace," I insisted.

"You'll have time," my mother assured me.

Again I was asked which of my parents I wanted to travel with the baby up to the nursery to be weighed and measured and bathed and which of them I wanted to remain with me. In their surgical gowns and masks they held her together, both of them beaming at me like I'd never seen. I said, "Don't you both want to go with the baby?"

They nodded eagerly. I was only going to have a bit more surgery, and it was not the exciting part. Besides, I was getting a marguerita and going to la la land for a while legally. Both Dale and Ginny accompanied our nine pound, one half ounce, 22" tall perfectly healthy baby girl to the nursery.

When I awoke sometime later in a recovery room of sorts, it was the nurse from the garage sale I saw first. She had indeed given Olivia her first bath. She handed the squeaky clean baby to me and my father, mother, brother, friend LuAnne, and a few hours later teacher friends Craig and Stacey who had all joined me to celebrate the miraculous birth of this baby girl.

It was hours later, Sunday evening when we were finally alone and I was nursing her that I discussed names with my daughter. I ran through the short list while she busily latched on and ate. I said, "How do you like Isabella Grace?" she kept eating. "Emily Grace?" still no response. "Sarah Grace?" nothing. "Merideth Grace?" still nothing. "Victoria Grace?" she frowned, perhaps worried as was I that it would be shortened to Vicki and therefore land on my long refrigerator list (no offense intended at all – I am simply not a nickname person). When I said "Olivia Grace" she smiled. "You like that one?" I asked her. Then I ran through the list all over again and got the exact same reaction. "Okay," I told her. "Olivia Grace it is, and you can never complain to me that you hate your name because YOU chose it."

Later that night, my exhausted parents returned to the hospital along with a very chagrined Jaime who had called and asked our father where I was and why hadn't I left a note…. And he told her, "Have you tried the hospital?"

"NO!" she screamed.

"Yes," he smiled. "We'll be right there to take you to them, coach."

When they walked in the door, along with my 80-something maternal grandmother, Olivia was asleep in the glass basinet by my bed. I told them I would like to introduce them all to someone, and they smiled as I said, "Please welcome to the world Miss Olivia Grace Hillard." My mother actually clapped her hands together in glee.

"I was hoping that was the name you'd choose. I wouldn't let Jaime talk about it because we were afraid you would get tired of it before she was born."

Olivia Grace Hillard is the answer to my bedside prayer. She is the greatest joy and miracle I've ever been a part of, and I knew right away that she belonged not just to me, but to all of us. She was a miracle to all of us.

My father's Thanksgiving prayer that year still rings in my head, "Thank you Father, this Thanksgiving Day for the gift of this dear child, Olivia Grace and even more so for giving us back our daughter, better than ever."

Chapter Thirty-three - Still More Miracles:

"Babies get most of their food on their faces, their hair, their ears, and similar places; and we adults are always berating them, when instead, we ought to be imitating them... And then, although we'd be messy at dinner, at least we'd be a whole lot thinner." (Mark Twain)

"and you shall know the truth, and the truth shall make you free." (John 8:32)

Throughout my pregnancy, there were two staples I absolutely craved. One was pickles and the other was Haagen Daas vanilla ice cream with my own, terribly rich chocolate sauce poured liberally over the top (and you wondered how 105 pound me could gain 71 pounds?).

One afternoon, before moving into our home from the apartment in Chandler, I came in from school and went straight to the refrigerator. I just knew I had a few slices of dill pickle left in my oversized jar. Imagine my horror at finding the jar devoid of pickles. I never put away empty containers; but apparently I had. I shrugged to myself and just drank the brine. When I phoned my mother later and told her what I had done, she grimaced quite audibly. About 45 minutes later I heard a light tapping at my door and there stood my mother, proffering a Costco sized gallon-jar of dill pickles. She had been trying to feed me for a few years, and she just couldn't stand the thought of me drinking pickle juice.

Later in the pregnancy, it was getting hot, April was upon us, and I was a humpback whale in cute matching cotton outfits my mother appliquéd with watermelons, bunnies, pumpkins at Halloween (why is it that maternity clothes have to resemble those we later purchase for our offspring?). Anyway, I had been teaching all day, my ankles were swollen, I was hot and I was tired. I came home (by then my folks and I had been renovating a home for the baby and me as they couldn't stand the thought of their grandchild being raised in an apartment). I can't really blame them; by then the place was not exactly filled with great memories.

Anyway, that afternoon I just needed some ice cream (vanilla). My freezer was empty. Too tired to do much about it, I waddled back to the couch and said to God, "Okay God. You have worked many miracles in my life, so what I'm about to ask of you is relatively minor in comparison to saving my life, giving me this baby and more friends than I can count. I just want a half-gallon of vanilla ice cream. If you love me at all, just send me some vanilla ice cream." After that I dozed for probably a half hour. I was awakened by the doorbell, which was unusual at 4:00 in the afternoon. I hoisted myself off of my comfy sofa and answered the door.

To my astonishment stood a man in a yellow uniform, pamphlet in hand and huge yellow freezer truck parked on my curb.

"Hello ma'am," he said. "I am Dan from the Schwann Corporation, and we are in your neighborhood giving away free half gallons of ice cream. We have 54 delicious flavors."

I smiled at him and said, "You may think you're Dan from Schwann's, but you are the angel God just sent to answer my prayer for a half gallon of vanilla ice cream to come to me."

He started to protest that I should really read the list. Bing cherry was excellent, he noted, as was fudge swirl.

"I'll just take the vanilla," I smiled. "You see, I'm nine months pregnant and I've been teaching teenagers how to write all day. I just want the vanilla."

Dan went to his heavenly truck and returned with two half gallons for me; one was vanilla, the other Bing cherry. To keep him happy, I accepted them both. I also continued to order from my yellow angel deliveryman every month for the next three years. If I'm anything, I am loyal, especially when miracles are involved.

Chapter Thirty-four - My death:

> *"Conceit is a queer disease. It makes everyone sick except the person who has it." (Elmer G. Leterman)*

> "Therefore I say to you, all things for which you pray and ask, believe that you have received them, and they shall be *granted* you." (Mark 11:24)

I recently read the best-selling account of Pastor Don Piper's death and visit to heaven. I couldn't wait to finish the book so I could write to him and compare our "Cliff's Notes" of the experience. I saw many, many parallels. Here is my letter to him:

Dear Don:

I finished reading your book last night. I, too, have been to heaven and NO ONE has ever been able to convince me it was a hallucination or too much medication on the operating table or some cell death in my brain. I've experienced all of those, I'm sure, but like you, heaven for me was the most real and VIVID experience of my life. I remember the music, the beautiful people who greeted me, the smell (sort of -- though I yearn for it) and my "flying" hug to Jesus. I said to them, as the operating room just sort of unfolded in layers like an onion and I was there, "Wow! You're really here!"

Someone said, "You knew that."

I replied, "Yes, I did. But it never hurts to gather evidence."

They all laughed and together we rejoiced. In my experience, my friend Eleanor who died at 84, a kid named Marty from my hometown who drowned at age eight, my uncle who died of cancer at 38, as well as a host of others whom I knew but cannot today name, in heaven, were all 33 (the age of Christ when he arrived there -- I'm thinking it must be the perfect age of spiritual maturity or just a very nice age to be forever -- certainly better than my current 46). I was a teacher at the time and I came back because one of the people there in heaven asked me, "What about Olivia?" (my then five-month-old daughter).

I just KNEW she would be joining us in a few moments and said as much. Someone, probably the outspoken Eleanor said, "Yes, but it won't feel like that to her. She didn't come to earth to spend the next 80 years without her mama."

I could then hear, from very far away, thin strained voices calling my name and screaming at me to breathe. The doctor and his nurse, doing what was to be a simple procedure and the last in a series of 11 operations at that time to remove skin grafts from the arm I nearly lost (you'll have to wait for me to finish my book for the whole story, or maybe recommend me to your publisher so I can get this thing rolling, finally) were Mormon, and he had been prattling away about the "truth" of LDS before I left his rather droll company. I looked to Jesus and said, "Don't make me leave."

He said it would be my choice.

I said, "I choose to stay, then."

I could hear them calling to me from the anthill of earth and knew without doubt that the entire POINT of earth is that we learn to love one another and God. My father was a minister my entire life (he still marries and buries people), and I played on the Bible Bowl team at the national tournament as a kid. But never was the whole concept made so clear and so simple to me. I knew I had to return to the anthill for my daughter, but told them all, "Save my place, do you hear me?" They laughed again.

Just that fast I was back in the sterile room feeling electricity pulse through my body as they shocked me. By the way, the nurse was the doctor's twin sister I later learned. I thought they KNEW where I had been, and came back bubbling over with it. Then I told them, "I saw Jesus. He held me. It was the best hug I've ever felt. And come to think of it, I did not see Joseph Smith nor Brigham Young, though I think Emma Smith and Brigham's first wife may have been there." They were not amused.

My mother was holding the baby and waiting in the lobby for me. The surgery ran almost two hours LONGER than they had explained it to her, the office having closed at noon that day (a Friday in early Oct, 1996). She said the nurse had gone in and out and about 12:30 went in, slammed the door and never again stepped out. I think that is when I went into respiratory arrest and clearly, my heart had stopped beating (though I have no memory of pain or death -- only arriving in heaven, free of grafts and scars and pain). I ran to my mother (the doctor was SO discombobulated that he had left IN the IV -- they NEVER do that, especially considering my history) and told her breathlessly where I'd been. She knows me and knew I was telling the truth. She said I radiated with it.

We later found burns or bruises in round discs on my chest and ribs where they had shocked my body back to life. They told my mother nothing had happened; that I must have had an adverse reaction to the anesthesia.

At my follow up appointment a week later I was still bubbling over with the joys of heaven and went to the receptionist, with whom I'd become quite close over the months and asked her if she'd heard what had happened to me.

Her reply still amuses me. "Nothing happened to you, and we're not allowed to talk to you about it."

I asked, "If nothing happened to me, why can't you talk about it?" She gave me the blank stare Mormons often give when confronted with absolute truth.

I was depressed for weeks upon my return. I adored and still adore my child. I loved teaching and cared absolutely for each 17- and 18-year old I taught, as well as the adults and fellow teachers I taught at ASU. (I have great credentials and my calling was to teach -- I got MS seven years ago, however, and cannot bear the daily regimen of teaching without losing my vision.) I told everyone about heaven! But I remember asking my students one afternoon what was wrong with the lights in our classroom. They said "Nothing. They look just like they always do, fluorescent."

To me, the whole world looked dark, like I was wearing UV-rated sunglasses. It was the brightness of heaven I missed; and I didn't even go inside the brightest part. I seemed to know that if I stepped inside THAT pure light, I could not return. And Olivia did need ME. So, it turns out, did several people who were dying or about to die and asked for me to come to them and tell my experience. So did one of my senior boys who sat and wept after the class where I told them the whole of my story.

A word here about my dear mother. I don't know how she found the strength and how together we endured the agony, but the surgeon had been so flustered that he had hurriedly closed the left arm, leaving a section about one inch wide and seven inches long that had to be pulled close together in order for the new skin to knit together. He installed blue rubber bands and each day following that fateful surgery, my mother untied them and pulled them just a bit closer together. Each touch of the banding was torture to my open wounds, and as you might imagine, not the best method of plastic surgery for one prone to keloid healing anyway. I was left with scars worse that the skin grafts had ever been. And, I saved doggedly and paid the nearly $12,000 to HAVE those repair operations and implants as they were not covered by insurance, but were considered, "cosmetic." I won't even launch into a diatribe on that issue. Suffice it to say, that with firm love and logic, my mother knitted together my open wounds and loved me, together with my father, just as I was. I was going to be a quilted bear, criss crossed with scars for the rest of my life. It took years to accept that I had caused such damage to the body God had so carefully prepared for me, one that had served me so well most all of my life (and still does, if the onlooker, like Eric, has no peripheral vision).

The best though was a Jewish professor with whom I was team-teaching a Research class at ASU. Her mother had died several years prior to me and she felt certain she would never again see her mother. I didn't know her well at the time, but I put my hands on hers and said, "Oh Arlene. You're wrong about that." I told her everything. Two nights later, in the middle of the night, she called me and accused me of reading a Spanish novel of which I'd never heard. I don't speak more than three words of Spanish. Apparently, one of the main characters in her book had had a NDE (near-death experience) and found everyone in heaven to be, you got it, 33. The hairs all over her body were standing on end and we've had lunch together every year since that class. Believing Jesus is the Messiah is a tough one for her, both ethnically and religiously, but Arlene now believes that the Rabbi does not hold all the answers and yearns for the day she will reunite with her mother and KNOW the truth.

I don't know what the Mormon surgeon's office decided about the whole event. They were terrified I would sue them. Are they insane? Why would I sue them for sending me to Paradise?

Like you, I have absolutely no fear of death or serial killers, rapists or drive-by shootings. I can't wait to go back and hope I get a room near yours so we can sing together and dance and share a flying hug with Our Lord.

Faithfully yours,

Judith Ann Hillard

Chapter Thirty-five - The Cockroach People:

"Character is simply habit long continued."
(Plutarch)

"Beloved, I pray that in all respects you may prosper and be in good health, just as your soul prospers." (3 John 2)

My former student had disappeared again, but this time she'd been gone for a couple of days. She was only 21, had dropped out of college about a year before, and had most recently been living with her parents (well, after she ran away from her second treatment center, that is). Her mother was beside herself with worry and fear, as this was her baby, and she was lost. Michelle was really lost, more than my mother could possibly know. You see, Michelle was addicted to cocaine. Perhaps only I knew just how lost my student was. Five years before, I too had been addicted to cocaine. And after my young prodigy saw the underbelly side of life from my point of view, it never occurred to any of us that she would want to go there herself. Five years before, it was she who tried so hard to save my life. She so wanted me to live, that once or twice, I actually prayed that I would for Michelle's sake alone. During those weeks and even months of my life, I was nearly dead and I did not care.

Now, I didn't know exactly where Michelle was, but I had a good idea what the place looked like and what the inhabitants with her looked like. Michelle was beneath the surface of the earth surrounded by the cockroach people, probably in a house or apartment surrounded by suspicious but not-wanting-to-get-involved neighbors.

The call came early one morning from the wife of a man Michelle had met in treatment. He, too, had been gone for several days. But the wife, about 8 ½ months pregnant, had a good idea where he was, and felt fairly certain that Michelle was with him. We quickly gathered ourselves into a search and rescue team. Michelle's father called a friend of his who was the chief of police in a suburb of Phoenix. He instructed us to find the place and get Michelle out, then call in the appropriate city police department. We arranged to meet the pregnant wife and bring along my brother, who happened to have a black belt in a couple of different martial arts and a particular hatred for drugs.

What a force we made: the pregnant wife, we'll call her Angie, her two little girls, aged approximately two and four, neatly strapped into car seats in the back seat of their old car. The husband had of course absconded with the new red pickup truck whose payments were so far in arrears that it was due to be repossessed by the bank the following morning. Michelle's mother, armed with some juice boxes (as she was fairly certain we would find her daughter dehydrated) and some Kleenex (in case we didn't find her, I suppose, or in case we found her in worse shape than just thirsty); her father, behind the wheel of his squeaky clean four-wheel drive SUV, cell phone at the ready; my brother sitting silently beside me in the backseat, except for the occasional cracking of his knuckles and silent, rolling stretches of his muscular, black-belted shoulders; then there was me, probably the fiercest opponent in the car as we drew near the suspected address.

I despise the cockroach people. I know them too well. I know how compelling they can be, how lost, yet how dark and sinister they are, individually and collectively. And above all, I knew that they cared nothing for my student or one another. They each had but one goal: to obtain cocaine, and they would use whomever and whatever they had to in the singular purpose of securing more. And even when that happened, there was never enough.

We decided in the car that Michelle's mom and I should approach the house rather than her 6'2" father and my heavily muscled brother. We wanted to get inside in order to get Michelle out, not scare them to death before they opened the door. I grabbed her dad's cell phone and, with her mother right beside me, marched up to the front door. On the way up the ratty yard, past its short chain link fence I prayed aloud for God to arm us with soldier angels and the power we needed to free Michelle from the crack house and its occupants. There was the cabin part of a semi-truck parked crookedly in the driveway, many other cars up and down the street in front of this horrible house. We saw Michelle's blue pick-up parked sideways behind the semi and her friend's about-to-be repossessed red truck cleverly "hidden" in the backyard, alongside a garage converted into a guest house (though Martha Stewart had clearly never been there).

I called out in my loudest voice as I pounded on the front door, "We are Michelle's mother and teacher. We are holding a cell phone and a timer. The phone is programmed to call the police, the fire department, the Army, Navy, Air Force, and National Guard. All I have to do is hit send and the law will descend on you by land, air, and water. You have sixty seconds to send her out here. 59. 58. 57...."

The door inched open and an old, smelly, toothless guy said there was no Michelle inside the house. He tried to shut the door, but I stuck my foot in its path. "Pal, do you see that blue Toyota behind the big rig?" He did. "That would be my friend's car. She IS in there and I suggest you find and produce her soon. 46. 45. 44." He slammed the door.

Michelle's mom and I walked around to the side door and I kept right on counting. 39. 38. 37. Just then the door to the guest house swung open wide and four naked people ran out. One still had a tourniquet around his skinny arm. In fact, that was all he was wearing. We could see the dirty, striped mattresses on the floor in the room they'd just left. We could also see glass pipes, mirrors, razor blades, syringes, blood. You know, the usual stuff people keep in apartments. "Hey man, we don't know no Michelle. We don't know what goes on in that house."

I remained as did my friend's mother, immovable and resolute. "Have a bit of lockjaw, pal? Well, you better scramble through that dog door and find her, because once I press send, I don't think the law will care which house you came from. 28. 27. 26...."

Tourniquet man crawled through the doggie door into the filthy kitchen. I heard him say, "I don't know who's out here, but she has a bunch of cops and soldiers with her and they're busting in if someone named Michelle doesn't come out like now."

I kept counting down. 19. 18. 17. Michelle's mom kept praying quietly, holding tight to my hand. Suddenly people in varying amounts of clothing started jumping out the front windows. Before I got to 15, the front door swung open again and Michelle practically flew out before it was pulled tight again. She was some kind of mad, swearing at me and telling me these were her friends and I was offending them, and besides, she still had "stuff" inside.

I said, "If they're your friends, they'll save your 'stuff' for you." She flipped me off. We got her into the car, though it was not easy. Her friend Benjamin came out, saw his wife and children, and threatened to hit my brother if he took Michelle away.

Philip literally lifted the man off the ground and said, "Just give me a reason, Benjamin. Go ahead, throw the first punch." It was pretty clear, even to a loaded Benjamin that he was no match for a black belt in Karate, Judo, Jujitsu, etc.... I've watched my brother break piles of cinder block with his bare hands before he hit puberty. He is a grown man now and I think it took every ounce of his considerable strength not to kill Benjamin then and there with his bare hands. He set the man down and helped us force Michelle into the backseat of her father's SUV.

Michelle was still swearing and spitting and she smelled like open sewage. Her hair was greasy and wild, and her eyes, like those of her companions, were huge and black and empty. The occupants of the house started trickling out after I stopped counting. They gathered behind the sad, short fence and started yelling at me, calling me names. I looked into their eyes, or tried.

The lights were not on and no one was home. I call them the "cockroach people" as that is what they resembled. Skinny bodies, huge eyes, broken teeth, sinister expressions on their dirty faces, and no visible soul.

I have often wondered where our souls go when we are high on drugs. Do they hover, keeping watch over our pathetic bodies and addictions? Do they go to a safe place and just wait? I do know that my soul was not with my body when I used drugs. This may be why so much is hard or impossible to remember later, once the soul returns. This also makes this book so much more difficult to write. I am grateful today that I wrote during my addiction as well as throughout the many times I tried to stop. Hence I know I am telling you the truth. I told the cockroach people that they didn't have to keep living and dying like they were. "There is hope," I said as they continued to harangue me.

"You're an addict too! You're no better than us," one woman screamed at me.

I rolled up my sleeves and showed them my scars, though I'm not sure their dilated pupils could even focus on them. "That's right. I'm no better than any of you. But today, I don't have to live in filth and addiction and stench any longer. I pray you can break free of this deadly addiction, all of you." That quieted them for some reason. They stood in a line and watched us prepare to leave, obviously relieved that I had stopped counting.

Benjamin chose to stay behind, entrusting his very pregnant wife and children to us. My brother drove his family to their home. Michelle's mother moved into the front passenger seat beside her husband. I had no choice but to sit in the back, beside the wild animal that was then my charge, Michelle. She smelled so terrible that her dad's "new car" smell was powerfully and quickly overcome. I asked him if we couldn't just tie her to the roof rack until we got her home. "As tempting a thought as that is, I think we need to keep her belted in right where she is." We rolled down the windows, and although it was Phoenix, it was January and it was cold. As her dad drove away from the curb, I hit send on his phone. We didn't stick around to see how exactly the coast guard would arrive in the middle of the desert. I guess the Cockroach People had forgotten there was no ocean nearby.

We drove to Michelle's parent's home. It was not a small miracle that her elder sister, Janis, happened to be present when Michelle most desperately needed her. I stepped aside, exhausted, knowing God and his military had indeed been beside and behind her mother and me just an hour before that. I prayed they would stay with Michelle. Apparently, they did. Michelle willingly let Janis step her, first fully clothed and then stripped down to her skinny self, into the shower and rinse the filth and drugs from her clothes and skin and hair. She emerged about an hour later and ate some soup. Her mom and dad told me later that after she ate, she slept for several days. It took some time and a month in treatment, but Michelle did overcome her brief addiction to crack cocaine.

Last night, seven year later, Olivia and I attended the birthday party of Michelle's oldest child. She has three children. I had to smile as they all piled into my new, cool VW convertible and took it for several spins around the block and returned to their own four-bedroom house. They are healthy and beautiful and when I take the time to focus, I can feel the love flowing around and between them.

Chapter Thirty-six - Helping Others:

"I am ready to meet my Maker. Whether my Maker is prepared for the great ordeal of meeting me is another matter." (Sir Winston Churchill, eve of his 75th birthday)

"Who shall separate us from the love of Christ? Shall tribulation, or distress, or persecution, or famine, or nakedness, or peril, or sword?" (Romans 8:35)

Because I am involved not in a recovery group, but a group of healed people who have Overcome addiction, I am occasionally allowed the privilege of sharing my story with others and sometimes even helping them choose life over addiction. Let me state for the record here that many times the 12-step programs have saved and enriched my life. My hesitancy with them is that the higher power one must have to succeed can be anything. One member of my group calls them, therefore, the doorknob group. If a doorknob could keep me clean, I would not have had to die and nearly die so many times. It is only God who can heal us. God alone is our Higher Power. Today, I no longer fight nor question that His will is far wiser than mine, and He is far mightier than a mere white powder.

I still attend some 12-step meetings. And when my number is called (and it is not called very often) I share the truth of what I know. I don't say, "I choose to call my Higher Power God," as if it is up to me. I speak of the miracles the One True God has lavished upon me. I speak of a healing and of overcoming half a lifetime of addiction. I do not care if I am not a politically correct AA'er. It is the truth. Today, I do not fear speaking it.

As a part of my 12-step program, I made a list of all persons and institutions I could think of that I had harmed and became willing to make amends to them all. This I have certainly not yet accomplished. It will probably take a lifetime and then some to do so and perhaps this book will at least help explain the insanity that for so long infested my being.

Part of a self-inventory is listing the best things I've done. Aside from producing Olivia, my list includes poems and family "tests: seeking to preserve family lore and tradition," teaching, loving and nurturing stray animals (mostly cats and with a lot of help from my friend, Carmen), and sharing myself and my experiences with others.

When I was asked to list my character strengths, I honestly could not think of ANY. My two sponsors (no one would agree to sponsoring me alone, as I was edgy material at best with a not-too-successful track record) suggested several: my ability to be honest, my earnestness in getting better, my eagerness to find the truth and the answers to my disabling addiction. These are just a few of the many things they named. They mentioned my humor, my willingness to love and be loved, my humility and generosity. I had never thought of these things as strengths in my character. I'd just always thought I WAS a character and people forgave my weaknesses, if they could, because I was somewhat charming. Today I remember that every city has its mansion district and its ghetto. I am no different.

Through the 12-step program, I began to make amends to those I had hurt. One of my amends was to the headmaster who had fired me seven years earlier. I wasn't sure why I felt a burning desire to write to him, a man I hardly had the chance to know and who certainly never had the chance to really know me. His answer to my letter provided the answer to that question. He was just weeks from retirement when my letter arrived, and was thrilled to know that I had survived and what exactly had been wrong with me. Here is my letter to him:

11 October 2001

Mr. James Callahan
Head of School
The Prep school

Dear Mr. Callahan:

This letter is so long overdue, that I am almost embarrassed to be writing it. I hope you will understand that my doing so is an important part of my continued recovery, and will forgive its tardiness and recognize instead its sincerity and the humility with which I offer it to you.

Just before I joined your faculty in September of 1994, I had begun using cocaine. At first it started as an occasional thing, a way to work longer and think more clearly. Very quickly after you met me, my addiction to it grew exponentially. I lost more and more weight, more and more ability to think and reason correctly. I had befriended a third year resident at Penn during that awful period of my life and he instructed me that snorting cocaine was too damaging to my sinuses and I should, as Sigmund Freud and this young man himself did, inject the drug. Stupidly and sadly, I agreed to try this. Very quickly, I was in a desperate condition.

The very best thing you could have done for me was exactly what you did: fire me. It was a devastating loss for me, but relieved me of all the excuses I had left for not going home to Arizona and getting help. That winter I was able, finally, to board a plane (with the help of Chase and Phoebe) and travel to my parents in Phoenix. We went straight from Sky Harbor Airport to Good Samaritan Hospital, where I spent the next seven weeks of my life getting better. I weighed 84 pounds and had a hemoglobin count of two. It is impossible that I did not die; yet this letter is evidence that indeed, I did not. In perhaps my darkest hour, I got down on my knees that had been too proud to bend in that direction in a very long time and cried out to God, "Please, if you can still hear me, just give me a reason to live. I don't even care what it is, but without it, I know I cannot keep doing it."

God did hear my prayer. That was July 17, 1995. Since that time, I have not ever felt the need to invade my body with drugs. A year later I was teaching once again, this time in the same school district I had attended as a teenager. I was the proud, healthy mother of a 9 lb, 1/2 oz. baby girl named Olivia Grace Hillard. Grace being God's gift we do not deserve but receive anyway. Clearly, God knew best how to heal what could not be healed; how to soothe what was so abrasive; how to embrace one who was so lost. Olivia is now five years old, bright and precocious, beautiful and healthy. When I left my home school district for a one-year leave of absence, I had been promoted to Staff Development Director of the entire district. I was able to return not only to my life, my soul, and my family, but also to my work ethic and the career to which I was well suited.

I am still trying to finish my dissertation after all of these years. So much of life took precedence over academia. During that year of my leave, I was diagnosed with multiple sclerosis. Since that time, I have been forced to live each day to its fullest. Some days my vision is impacted and other days I can't feel my legs or hands. Usually it is pain and spasticity in my neck and spine that causes me the most aggravation. But I live in a state of gratitude for the life that was restored to me. And for the new, precious life that was entrusted to me.

At this point, I am disabled by the MS, but comfortable enough to write and occasionally speak about my recovery. I spent the first 34 years of my life trying to be something like Mary Poppins (practically perfect in every way). And when I fell, I fell hard and fast. I was one of the lucky 3% of cocaine addicts who actually can and do recover. And with all of the many things I lost, including much of my skin, my savings account, my job, and some of my friends, I am so grateful that I have retained at least most of my thinking and reasoning skills and have been able to replace most of those other things.

My reason for writing you all of this detail is to try and explain to you why I was such a disappointment to the prep school. I was so sick, and my illness made it impossible for me to reach out and tell anyone the truth about what was wrong with me. I was virtually lost, and I did not know how to let anyone find me. I am so ashamed of the damage I did to my body and my soul, to my family and friends, and to each and every life there that I touched in those few months I was privileged to teach in your fine institution.

I want to apologize to you for the pain and agony I caused you and my fellow teachers as well as the students who cared for and worried about me. I am profoundly sorry that we found one another when I was at the lowest, scariest point in my life. If I had met you two years earlier or two years later, ours would have been a lasting and wonderful partnership as we worked together to educate some of the brightest, kindest, most thoughtful teenagers I have ever had the honor of knowing. If there is ever anything I can do to help you in your outreach to students about the horrors of even trying drugs, please ask. I know I cannot repay the damage I caused while there, but it is my sincerest hope that I can make amends for being such a disappointment to you. Perhaps this letter has been able to do that.

Humbly,

Judith Ann Hillard

My former headmaster wrote that he had several unanswered questions as he approached his impending retirement THAT spring. I had managed to answer one of the most nagging of his questions and quiet for him an unease he had known since he knew me. He thanked me for my candor and prayed with me for continued recovery and good health and congratulated me on arriving at parenthood. It was a circle completed; a wound healed. But like this writing, possible only in my willingness to first humble myself, roll up my sleeves (for me, this is HUGE), and *get out of God's way* as He began to market His miracles in my life.

One of my former students is struggling even now with a drug addiction that has nearly cost her everything: her marriage, her children, her job(s), her health, her sanity (or so she fears), her life. She has intentionally overdosed and then panicked in time to have her stomach pumped (not a fun experience, and I say so from just that – experience). She emails and occasionally calls me, attempting to reach out and then running away when I confront her with the steps SHE alone must take in order to repair her twisted world. Her words break my heart. How can this lovely, talented woman not know how special she is, how beloved by so many? She once wanted to be like me, when she was a teen and I her English teacher. Could she not have chosen another mentor? Why did she have to emulate me of all people? I pray for her throughout my waking hours and when my sleep is interrupted. I pray for her three children. I have offered to take them into my home and love them and give them the structure they now lack so painfully. I've offered to bring Kelly here too, as long as she is clean. She has not yet been able to satisfy my singular rule. I fear that she will succeed in killing herself. I fear for her and for her children. I fear for her parents who are frightened out of their minds over their star athlete, straight-A student, most-likely-to-succeed daughter. I weep for the girl she once was and still see her in the woman she now is. I wish I could have told her the truth about me when I was her teacher and track coach. But she was 15, 16, 17. I just could not speak to a child of the pain and agony I had already cost myself, long before the cocaine. I too was a prescription drug addict. I kept that largely to myself. Unfortunately, I graduated to the very thing I KNEW I would never be: a junkie. I have walked where Kelly now walks. I have fallen there so many times. By the grace of God and a thousand miracles, I no longer travel that road. I long for my student to join me on this one.

My Dearest Kelly:

You are scaring me so badly. Believe me when I type this in caps and know that I am not yelling at you, but relating:

I KNOW HOW YOU FEEL. I KNOW IT EXACTLY. I HAVE TRIED SO HARD TO CONVEY THAT IN MY BOOK. I AM WRITING LIKE A MADWOMAN. PLEASE KEEP

READING. PLEASE KEEP BREATHING. YOU ARE NOT
INSANE. YOU ARE AN ADDICT. SO AM I. YOU ARE IN
THE COMPANY OF MILLIONS OF PEOPLE WHO SHARE
THAT DISEASE. THERE IS NO OTHER DISEASE. IT IS THE
DISEASE THAT MAKES US CRAZY. THE SANITY
RETURNS WHEN WE FINALLY LET GO OF THE
ADDICTION.

Yes, you need to be with me every Friday night. You need
to bring your children here, to my home, and let them get used to
it. You need to get OUT OF your neighborhood, AWAY FROM
THOSE DR'S who believe they are HELPING you. They are
killing you, unawares. Your parents can't even help you (or the
kids) right now. You all need distance and time in order to heal.

Kelly, don't give up. The miracle may be there now, just waiting
for the last disaster. Don't be afraid to ask for a miracle. You need
one.

I love you too. I am no longer your teacher. I am your friend.
You need one of those as well. You are NOT alone,

Judith Ann

Chapter Thirty-seven - Overcoming and Peace:

> *"There is no difficulty that enough love will not conquer; no disease that enough love will not heal; no door that enough love will not open; no gulf that enough love will not bridge; no wall that enough love will not throw down; no sin that enough love will not redeem... It makes no difference how deeply seated the trouble may be; how hopeless the outlook; how muddled the tangle; how great the mistake. A sufficient realization of love will dissolve it all...If only you could love enough, you would be the happiest and most powerful being in the world."* (Emmet Fox)

"Greater is he that is in you, than he that is in the world." (I John 4:4)

I have been a believer almost every hour of my life. My favorite game as a child was to turn the white vinyl footstool on end and use it as my pulpit. I would pull all the dining room chairs around so they faced my pulpit, and seat my dolls and stuffed animals in them. I preached to my captive audience, served them communion and prayed. When I got a little older than two or three, I found it delighted my grandparents to attend "Judi's church." I also learned then how to pass the offering plate. Smile. They were what the good book calls "cheerful givers."

It has been many years since I was baptized by my father (I was nine, and it was Easter Sunday night). I was on fire for God as a junior high school student. And you know the rest of the Mary Poppins story. I know beyond doubt that I have been snatched from the jaws of death many times. I love God and adore His Son, but would still not call myself one of the "crazed-again" Christians. I am human. I still stumble. I still question. I still cry out to God (mostly in the car or in the shower, when I feel most alone) and ask WHY? "Why must I carry these ugly, hideous scars? Who is ever going to love me again or find me attractive?

Am I supposed to live all alone my whole life (after Olivia leaves home, which is happening much faster than I ever dreamed it would)? Why didn't you just take me home all of the thousands, or at least hundreds of times I could not breathe, or my heart pounded above 220 times per minute? Why did I have to be a drug addict? I would much rather be a politician. (But I inhaled.) Will I ever be able to work again? Will anyone ever invite me to speak to teenagers again? Am I here on earth simply to help others die? I know you gave me a reason to live, but remind me again what it is!"

Quietly, over the months and years, I got my answer. I have so often described myself as The Lone Ranger. I even have his watch. I've also called myself "the woman at the well." Too long I have felt alone, and this is true only because I isolated myself from people and from the flow and dignity of life. I have tripped too often on this particular stone (no pun intended, honestly) and I am sick to death of it. I may trip on others and certainly will stumble; but never again will I fall into addiction. This I have FINALLY overcome.

I may still be the woman at the well, but today I drink from those waters in the company of millions of others who have recovered from this deadly, evil disease. Today I am one among many standing at the well. Today I have company.

"Greater love has no one than this, that one lay down his life for his friends. You are My friends...." (John, ch. 15: 13-14) I always thought I'd have to give a kidney, or be Sidney Carton in *A Tale of Two Cities* to display this great a love to others. Today I don't have the life I always thought I would have. I have set aside that dream, that wrong direction and having survived the war, let God lead me to share myself HONESTLY with others. Now I understand that for me, laying aside my Mary Poppins costume and face and being real is the greater love. Today I pray that young people will NOT emulate me; but rather, will be saved from pain and degradation because I told them the truth about drug addiction. It is a far more powerful message than Nancy Reagan's "Just Say No." I'm sorry if that offends anyone. But the people who "just say no" have clearly never tried drugs. They simply don't know what they're talking about. Teenagers know this, they have an uncanny ability to sniff out deception. When I am privileged to share my story with them, they listen and sometimes cry and always ask me a boatload of tough questions. I answer them honestly. It is not easy. That is, for me, greater love.

Today I try to be a blessing to others. Some days that is a much tougher goal than others. Like you, I'm sure, I have days when I am absolutely inspired to simply give what I can, be it hope to a weary sales clerk, or a sandwich to a hot, skinny person standing with a hand-lettered sign on a corner in my city, or a few dollars to one of my sisters who has multiple children and massive grocery bills. I was recently able to send a check to one sister and leave some cash beneath the pillow of another. Of course, they both wrote and thanked me generously. That is not the point. The point is to give because Olivia and I have received so much we just HAVE to give back. God is kind to us, especially when I am notably kind to others in a quiet way.

Today, I am healed. I am delivered. I have experienced the unmerited favor of God in the form of Grace. My family has forgiven me and begun slowly to trust in me again. Olivia no longer wishes she slept somewhere else, and sometimes wants to sleep with me not because she's afraid I'll die in the night, but because she is a little girl and she wants to be near her mama. Today I find joy in that and allow her to do so, though I know I'll be kicked several times and rolled into and be without covers much of the night.

I am certainly not perfect. I still take the hamster turds of life and turn them into mountains of elephant dung. I rarely flow with too much traffic. But today I am more inclined to be patient with myself and that makes me kinder to others. I count to ten before raising my voice to Olivia. Sometimes I have to count to ten times ten. But living with a drug-free mom with foibles is certainly better than living with a drug addicted mom who notices almost nothing.

I have dwelt too long in darkness; today I walk in the light. I am safe. I am loved. I am a child of God. I am healthy and living my life, not hastening its end. Through the love and power of a God I cannot yet understand, I was and am saved. Today I have hope. I pray that as you read this testimony, you feel the power of hope return to your life, no matter what or who around you is caught up in addiction and destruction and death. No matter how hopeless you feel, may you reach up from your own unique pain and take the hand of the only true source of strength and power and love, and may you run and jump into His mighty arms and remain there forever, close to me.

Back in Samaria: "But an hour is coming, and now is, when the true worshipers shall worship the Father in spirit and truth; for such people the Father seeks to be His worshipers. God is spirit; and those who worship Him must worship in spirit and truth. The woman said to Him, 'I know that Messiah is coming (He who is called Christ); when that One comes, He will declare all things to us.' Jesus said to her, 'I who speak to you am *He…*' So the woman left her waterpot, and went into the city, and said to the men, 'Come, see a man who told me all the things that I have done; this is not the Christ, is it?' (John 4:23-29) There she was, a woman, a sinner, not born into wealth or position or prominence, and she went on to be one of the great champions of the Savior. He touched her life and made her whole. I know this to be true; He also touched mine.

XXXXXXXXXXXXXXXXXXXXXX

Made in United States
Orlando, FL
24 June 2022